HISTORY OF ENGLISH

Second Edition

'This second edition of Jonathan Culpeper's *History of English* retains the outstanding features of the first edition – it covers all the topics relevant to a study of the history of English. In addition, the second edition brings with it a new rigour and a fuller and more careful and detailed account of, in particular, spelling and speech sounds, grammar, dialects and standardisation. I congratulate the author on the improvements made in this second edition.'

Sue Powell, University of Salford, UK

Routledge Language Workbooks provide absolute beginners with practical introductions to core areas of language study. Books in the series provide comprehensive coverage of the area as well as a basis for further investigation. Each Language Workbook guides the reader through the subject using 'hands-on' language analysis, equipping them with the basic analytical skills needed to handle a wide range of data. Written in a clear and simple style, with all technical concepts fully explained, Language Workbooks can be used for independent study or as part of a taught class.

History of English:

• examines the history of the English language in order to explain the English that is used today
• introduces key linguistic concepts
• provides 'discussion points' to generate debate
• encourages readers to think critically about the subject
• involves readers in collecting and analysing their own data
• contains a 'mini-corpus' of texts, used for exercises and to illustrate points raised in the commentary

The second edition has been revised and updated throughout, and includes new commentaries, maps and figures, as well as references to recommended internet resources. Whilst maintaining the accessibility for the beginner, the level of the entire book has been raised by the addition of much more detail, a greater focus on theories and controversies, and a clearer route to key works in the field.

Jonathan Culpeper is a senior lecturer in the Department of Linguistics and English Language at Lancaster University.

LANGUAGE WORKBOOKS

Series editor: Richard Hudson

Books in the series:

HISTORY OF ENGLISH

Second Edition

JONATHAN CULPEPER

Routledge
Taylor & Francis Group

LONDON AND NEW YORK

First published 1997

This edition first published 2005
by Routledge
2 Park Square, Milton Park, Abingdon, Oxon OX14 4RN

Simultaneously published in the USA and Canada
by Routledge
270 Madison Ave, New York, NY 10016

Routledge is an imprint of the Taylor & Francis Group

© 2005 Jonathan Culpeper

Typeset in Galliard and Futura by
Florence Production Ltd, Stoodleigh, Devon
Printed and bound in Great Britain by
TJ International Ltd, Padstow, Cornwall

British Library Cataloguing in Publication Data
A catalogue record for this book is available from the
British Library

Library of Congress Cataloging in Publication Data
Culpeper, Jonathan, 1966–
    History of English/Jonathan Culpeper. – 2nd ed.
        p. cm. – (Language workbooks)
    Includes index.
    1. English language – History.   2. English language –
    History – Problems, exercises, etc.   I. Title.
    II. Series.
    PE1075.C85 2005
    420′.9–dc22   2004028640

ISBN 0–415–34183–3 (hbk)
ISBN 0–415–34184–1 (pbk)

CONTENTS

ACKNOWLEDGEMENTS

While I have made wide-ranging changes to the text of the first edition in producing the second, the essence of the original is still there. Consequently, I am again indebted to all those individuals who helped me produce that first edition. Regarding the second, I would like to thank: Julian Swindell for dropping everything, in order to create the Scandinavian placename maps in Unit 1, and Chris Kutler for allowing us access to his placename database; Willem Hollmann for his sharp commentary on Unit 2; Gerry Knowles for discussions about aspects of Unit 9; and Merja Kytö for help with Text 5 in the mini-corpus and for generally raising my 'text awareness'. Finally, I would like to express my gratitude to all those scholars from around the world who sent me feedback on the first edition. This feedback has been decisive in shaping the second edition. Needless to say, if I ignored anybody's advice, I have only myself to blame.

Sources for Appendix IV

Text 1: from a facsimile of the *Peterborough Chronicle*, in Dennis Freeborn's *From Old English to Standard English* (London: Macmillan, 1992). Text 2: from *A Middle English Reader*, edited by O.F. Emerson (London: Macmillan, 1905). Text 3: from *The Prologues and Epilogues of William Caxton*, edited by W.J.B. Crotch, (The Early English Text Society, London: Oxford University Press, 1928). Text 4: from a facsimile of the Public Record Office document SCI 59/5, in *The Cely Letters: 1472–1488*, edited by A. Hanham (Early English Text Society, London: Oxford University Press, 1975). Text 5: from the *Merrie Tales of Skelton* (1567), extracted from the *Corpus of English Dialogues 1560–1760* (Merja Kytö and Jonathan Culpeper). Text 6: from the Authorised Version of the English Bible (1611), edited by W.A. Wright (Cambridge: Cambridge University Press, 1909). Text 7: from a facsimile of the *Areopagitica* (Henston: Scholar Press, 1968). Text 8(c): from Mark

Sebba's *London Jamaican: Language Systems in Interaction* (London: Longman, 1993: 14).

Permissions

Text 8(a) is cited by kind permission of IMCO Group Ltd; Text 8(b) by permission of Cow & Gate Nutricia; and the extract in Appendix I, which is taken from *The Oxford English Dictionary* (2nd edn, 1989), by permission of Oxford University Press.

USING THIS BOOK

Students and teachers read this!

The commentary in this book aims to be clear, and to deliver an account that would be generally accepted by the scholarly community. However, as I make clear in Unit 2, no account is entirely free from controversy. The exercises and discussion points in the book are partly designed to air some of those controversies, as well as exemplifying *and* moving beyond the points made in the commentary. This book aims to involve readers as much as possible in conducting their own investigations. If you decide just to read the book and not actively do the exercises, that is fine, but do read and think through all parts of the book. 'Answers' to exercises are in Appendix V, but this Appendix does not include 'answers' that can be worked out by using a reference work (e.g. a dictionary), that involve you working on your own data or that ask you about your own language usage.

Some exercises will ask you to consult 'an etymological dictionary', by which is meant a dictionary that contains historical information, such as how a word was created and how its meaning might have changed. The best dictionary for the purpose is the *Oxford English Dictionary* (2nd edn, 1989) (hereafter, the *OED*) (available in many libraries, and also on the internet (www.oed.com), though not for free). Appendix I describes some key features of *OED* entries. If you have not got access to the *OED*, don't panic! Some of dictionaries derived from the *OED* (e.g. the *Compact OED*, the *Shorter OED*) will prove sufficient for basic work. Alternatively, you could try a specialist etymological dictionary, such as C.T. Onion's *Oxford Dictionary of Etymology* (Oxford: Clarendon Press, 1966) or E. Partridge's *Origins: A Short Etymological Dictionary of Modern English* (London: Routledge, 1966), though the range of words covered is not as great as in the *OED*. Also, the *American Heritage Dictionary of the English Language* (Boston, MA: Houghton Mifflin, 2000) is a good source of historical information, tracing – where possible

– words back to Proto-Indo-European. Moreover, it is available for free at www.bartleby.com/61 (persevere with the search engine!).

During the course of this book, you will be referred to specific texts in the 'mini-corpus' of texts in Appendix IV. Texts have been selected to illustrate some of the changes that have occurred in English, and, sometimes, they also present the views of commentators on the language. You could expand the range of texts, but beware of modern editions in which the language has been modernised or 'cleaned up'. An excellent source of texts, including numerous facsimiles and accurate transcriptions, is Dennis Freeborn's *From Old English to Standard English* (2nd edn) (London: Macmillan, 1998). Alternatively, there are considerable quantities of historical texts available on the internet. Digital images give you a real sense of the historical document, but they can be difficult to read and cannot be searched by a computer. Conversely, electronic transcriptions are relatively easy to read and can be searched (e.g. if you want to find examples of a particular word or structure, you can easily retrieve them with some retrieval software or even the 'find' facility in a word processor). However, a drawback is that transcriptions are dependent on the purposes and abilities of the transcriber. Historians, for example, typically 'tidy up' the punctuation and spelling, but these might be the very things the linguist is interested in. It is advisable to seek out resources primarily designed for linguists. Appendix VI suggests possible web-links.

At the end of every unit, you will find a number of follow-up readings for the topic of that particular unit. Frequently, you will be referred to the relevant pages in David Crystal's *Encyclopedia of the English Language* (2nd edn) (Cambridge: Cambridge University Press, 2003). This is comprehensive, clearly written and, moreover, widely available. For more detailed, and often more authoritative, accounts of the history of English, readings are suggested for specific topics at the end of each unit, and Appendix VII gives suggestions for general, supplementary and more advanced readings.

THE BIRTH OF ENGLISH

Clues in placenames

The most important factor in the development of English has been the arrival of successive waves of settlers and invaders speaking different languages. The history of placenames in Britain is closely connected to the presence of various languages at various points in time.

English does not originate in Britain, but can be traced back to the language of the various tribes in what is today's north-west Germany. If you had been standing in Britain 2,000 years ago, you would probably have heard a language more like modern Welsh. Today, we consider languages such as Welsh, Scottish Gaelic, Irish Gaelic and Breton to be 'Celtic' languages. Ancient Britain was inhabited by various Celtic-speaking tribes, of which the 'Britons' were one. Appendix II displays the Indo-European 'family tree' of languages. Note the Celtic branch. The idea is that languages grouped on particular branches have features in common. Thus, the Welsh word for English 'water' is *dyn*, while in Gaelic it is *duine* and in Breton *dan*. Moreover, the assumption here is that languages are related because they had a common ancestor. For Celtic languages, this is obviously Celtic. But there are no written records of Celtic – it is a hypothetical language reconstructed by linguists. For example, we can minimally infer that the Celtic word-form for 'water' consists of [d + vowel + n]. Ultimately, if we go back far enough (and well before surviving written records), the theory is that we arrive at a language, Indo-European, which is the common ancestor of all the languages in the tree.

As far as vocabulary is concerned, the impact of the Celtic languages on English has been minimal – a mere handful of words. Scholars have claimed that words such as *brock* (a badger) and *dun* (a dark greyish brown colour) have a Celtic heritage. The predominant Celtic legacy is in placenames, such as those below:

Cities: Belfast, Cardiff, Dublin, Glasgow, London, York
Rivers: Avon, Clyde, Dee, Don, Forth, Severn, Thames
Regions: Argyll, Cumbria, Devon, Dyfed, Glamorgan, Kent, Lothian

EXERCISE

1.1 Consider the list of placenames above. What areas of the British Isles seem to be well represented? Can you guess why this might be?

We cannot be totally sure what these placenames might have originally meant. Like many other placenames, they pre-date written records, which are preserved in significant quantities in English only from about AD 700. Indeed, the study of the history of placenames in general is characterised by careful reconstruction (and a bit of guesswork!). Apart from records, we can, for example, compare placenames with words in surviving Celtic languages or consider the geography of the places in question. Thus, we can make a reasonable guess about the meaning of the placename element 'pen' in the placename *Pendle*, because 'pen' in today's Welsh means a summit or top, and there is indeed a hill top at *Pendle*. Such detective work in tracing the history of words, whether placenames or any other type of word, is a matter of ETYMOLOGY. Etymology will be an important issue in both Units 4 and 5. The study of both placenames and personal names in particular is referred to by linguists as ONOMASTICS.

Etymology

Onomastics

The first notable group of invaders to join the Celtic-speaking tribes of Britain were the Romans, bringing Latin (check Latin on the family tree in Appendix II). Although Julius Caesar had raided Britain in 54 and 55 BC, it was not until AD 43, under Emperor Claudius, that the real occupation of Britain got under way. Lowland Britain (the midlands and south), which already had had some cultural and trading contact with continental Europe and Rome in particular, was taken over relatively swiftly, but today's Wales and northern England – the highland areas – took a generation, and the invasion ground to a halt at Carlisle, where Hadrian's Wall was built to keep out tribes (e.g. the Picts) further to the north (i.e. in what we would think of as Scotland today). In the north of England, not only was the terrain more difficult but there was a lack of people to do business with, and so a 'military zone' was set up. In the lowlands to the south, there was a more highly developed system of aristocratic leaders, attracted by Roman culture and willing to do business. The result was deep societal divisions in the British Isles. The survival of Celtic placenames in some areas (see Exercise 1.1, p. 2) must partly reflect the lack of domination and/or assimilation of Romans in those areas.

The Romans often Latinised existing Celtic placenames, rather than inventing completely new names. *London* is a Celtic placename, supposedly based on the personal name *Londinos*, meaning 'the bold one'. It was made more like Latin by being changed to *Londinium*. Few placenames surviving today are straightforwardly based on single Latin words. If invading powers want a swift administrative transition, they do not change all the placenames, otherwise confusion will result. One example of complete change is *Catterick*, which apparently is derived from Latin *cataracta* 'a waterfall' (and there is a waterfall at *Catterick*). A less dramatic change is to add a placename element, of which the most notable from Latin are:

> *castra* = a camp, walled town (e.g. Lan*caster*)
> *portus* = port (e.g. *Port*smouth)
> *via strata* = paved way, a 'street' in a town (e.g. *Strat*ford)

In the above illustrative examples, only the first, *Lancaster*, has a Celtic element. 'Lan' is from the *River Lune*, and *Lune* is probably from Old Irish 'slán', meaning 'health-giving' (which wouldn't be my description of the river today!). The non-Latin and non-Celtic elements *mouth* and *ford* of the other examples, *Portsmouth* and *Stratford*, have a Germanic background.

The English language has its roots in the language of the second wave of newcomers – in the Germanic dialects of the tribes of north-western Europe (including areas of today's north-west Germany). Check English and its location in the family tree in Appendix II. Modern Germanic languages clearly have related words for English 'water' (e.g. Dutch 'water', German 'wasser', Swedish 'vatten'). These tribes, conventionally referred to as the Anglo-Saxons, entered Britain in the year AD 449, after the Romans had withdrawn in AD 410. At least that is what the standard histories say, drawing their inspiration from Bede, a monk at Jarrow in Northumberland, who completed his ecclesiastical history of the English people, the *Historia Ecclesiastica Gentis Anglorum*, in 735 (the surviving early eleventh-century manuscript can be seen at: http://image. ox.ac.uk/show?collection=corpus&manuscript=ms279b, and a translation can be found at: http://www.ocf.org/OrthodoxPage/reading/St. Pachomius/bede.html). According to Bede, three tribes – Angle, Saxon and Jutish – were initially invited in by the British king Vortigern, to help fight off the Picts to the north. Eventually, they became discontented with the deal offered by the Britons, so they helped themselves to British territory. Bede follows this with an apocalyptic account of mass murders, buildings being razed to the ground and refugees. Map 1.1 shows where these tribes are thought to have come from (there is particular uncertainty about the location of the Jutes).

Bede's account, however, is unreliable. Note he was writing 400 years after the event. Moreover, histories are selective interpretations, written by writers with their own agendas. Bede's claims about specific tribes invading in a purposeful and warrior-like manner would help create a heroic Anglo-Saxon history behind which the various tribes and kingdoms of Briton could unite. Placename evidence seems to suggest that there were identifiable tribes. The Angles appear to have settled in and given their name to what is now *East Anglia* (comprising *Norfolk* = 'north folk' and *Suffolk* = 'south folk'), and also spread to *Mercia* (the Midlands) and further north to *Northumbria* ('north (of the) Humber', and south-east Scotland). The Saxons appear to have remained in the south, as evidenced by the area names *Sussex* ('south saxons'), *Essex* ('east saxons'), *Middlesex* ('middle saxons') and the old name for the south-west *Wessex* ('west saxons') (Wessex extended from Sussex to Devon and as far north as Gloucestershire; its most famous capital was Winchester). The Jutes seem to have remained largely in Kent and the Isle of Wight. However, it is possible that the terms 'Angle', 'Saxon' and 'Jute' were overlapping or even synonymous, not least of all because commentators nearer that time were inconsistent in their usage. Archaeological evidence does not support the idea of invading hordes, mass destruction and the Britons fleeing to the north and west. Many excavations suggest slow dilapidation of Romano-British buildings, and not sudden

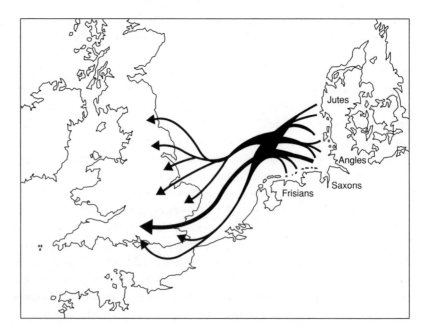

Map 1.1
Angle, Saxon and
Jute invasions

destruction. There was indeed some warfare and displacement of Britons, but there is also evidence that many Britons, particularly in the east, adopted the new prestigious Germanic culture, and there is evidence of intermarriage. Moreover, the Anglo-Saxons never got as far as the northern and western extremes of Britain. The Celtic languages – notably Cornish, Welsh, Irish Gaelic and Scottish Gaelic – proceeded relatively independently of English in what are today Cornwall, Wales, Ireland and Scotland. Each established its own literary tradition, and, excepting Cornish, which died out in the eighteenth century, are living languages today.

Records suggest that the Anglo-Saxons referred to themselves as *Englisc* or *Ænglisc* (derived from the name of the Angles) from the ninth century, and a little later used the term for their language. Thousands of English placenames were created by the Anglo-Saxons in this early period. Common placename elements (with various spellings) include:

> *Byrig/burg* = fort (e.g. Canter*bury*, Edin*burgh*)
> *dun* = hill (e.g. Swin*don*)
> *feld* = open land (e.g. Maccles*field*)
> *ford* = river crossing (e.g. Ox*ford*)
> *tun* = farm, village (later developing into 'town') (e.g. E*ton*)
> *ing* = place of (e.g. Claver*ing*)
> *ingas* = followers of (e.g. Hast*ings*, Read*ing*)
> *ham* = settlement, homestead (e.g. Nor*tham*)
> *hamm* = enclosure, land in a river bend (e.g. Chippen*ham*)

The final four elements give rise to potential difficulties in deciding the meaning of Anglo-Saxon placenames, since the modern placename spelling may not distinguish the original elements. In distinguishing *ham* and *hamm*, sometimes the only solution is to check the local landscape, in particular to see whether a river is present. This problem of spelling disguising the roots of words is in fact a more general problem in the study of placenames, and, indeed, in the study of words in general. We always need to be cautious in drawing conclusions, and try to trace the earliest possible forms.

Let's briefly consider how placename elements combine to form place-names. *Swindon*, for example, is created by combining the words *swine* (= pigs) and *dun* (= hill). This process of joining words to form other words is called COMPOUNDING. We will look at this process in more detail **Compounding** in Unit 5. Note that by investigating placenames we can learn about the culture and economy of the time. *Swindon* has a hill where, presumably, pig farming used to take place. A dominant trend in Anglo-Saxon place-names is that they take on the name of the tribal leader. For example, the first elements of the placenames *Macclesfield*, *Hastings* and *Chippenham* come from the personal male names *Mæccel*, *Hæsta* and *Cippa*. This trend highlights the fact that Anglo-Saxon society was patriarchal: power was concentrated in the hands of the leader, who, judging by placenames, was usually male (*Bœrma* of *Birmingham* is a rare exception).

In the ninth century, Britain saw the beginning of a third wave of newcomers – the Scandinavian Vikings, arriving from what would be today's Denmark, Norway and Sweden ('Scandinavian', as typically used in history of English books, does not include Finland). This is usually dated from the raid on Lindisfarne in Northumbria and the sacking of the monastery there in 793 (see some of the remarkable work carried out by the monks at: http://ibs001.colo.firstnet.net.uk/britishlibrary/controller/home (search on Lindisfarne)). Note that the fact that the Vikings were pagans, while most of the Anglo-Saxons were Christians (St Augustine had arrived in 597, spreading Christianity), would have made them seem more alien. These raids developed into continuous and spreading occupation, from about 851. This was finally halted when King Ælfred, the king of Wessex in the south-west, won a decisive victory over the Danish King Guthrum in 878. A treaty was concluded whereby the Danes stayed to the east of a line running roughly (the exact positioning of the line is controversial) from Chester to London, an area that later became known as Danelaw (see Map 1.2). While the Danish Vikings had been busy with the east and north of England, the Norwegian Vikings had invaded the northern and western isles of today's Scotland and the neighbouring parts of the Scottish mainland. They also tackled Ireland (founding the city of Dublin in 840), though they never completely colonised it. From about 900, the Norwegians in Ireland began to invade and settle in England, particularly the north-western areas.

In the tenth century, the Anglo-Saxons retrieved all the Danish territories south of the river Humber, even taking York, which had been a key Viking centre for many years (see http://www.jorvik-viking-centre.co.uk, for information about the Viking history of York and images of artefacts). But their fortunes were reversed in 991. Olaf Tryggvasson, king of part of Norway, defeated the Wessex King Æthelred II's army at Maldon in Essex (the poem *The Battle of Maldon* celebrates the event). Æthelred retaliated by ordering the massacre of Danes outside Danelaw. Unfortunately, one of the Danes who got killed was the Danish King's sister! The Danish King, Sveinn Forkbeard, arrived with a large army, and was in control of most of England, when he died in 1014. Æthelred returned from France (where he had fled), and began eliminating the Danes, upon which Sveinn's son, Canute, returned with a large army. (You may be wondering about the wisdom of this King Æthelred. He may be known to you as 'Ethelred the Unready'. 'Unready' is not thought to mean 'ill-prepared' but 'ill-advised', from 'un-ræd'.) A power-sharing agreement came about between Æthelred and Canute, but Æthelred died in 1016, leaving Canute in complete control. 'England' was part of the Danish Empire. But this situation did not last long: when Canute's son died in 1042, Æthelred's son, Edward (the Confessor), succeeded to the throne.

One important consequence of the Scandinavian invasions and settlement is that it had the effect of increasing linguistic differences between the north and the south of England. These differences are still apparent in today's dialects of English, and we will consider them further in Unit 9. One can also see the Scandinavian influence on placenames. Words derived from Scandinavian languages frequently appear in northern and north-eastern placenames – the shaded areas in Map 1.2. Common Scandinavian placename elements (with various spellings) include:

by = village (e.g. Kirk*by* or Kir*by*, Cros*by*)
thorp = village (e.g. Miln*thorpe*)
thwaite = glade, clearing (e.g. Hawthorn*thwaite*)

Interestingly, today's placenames ending *-thwaite, -scale, -slack, -gill* are almost exclusively in the north-west of England (Cumbria and North Lancashire) (see the left of Map 1.2), whereas those ending *-by* and *-thorp(e)* are largely in the north and east (see the right of Map 1.2). This reflects the fact that the first group is from an earlier form of Norwegian (Old Norse) and the second an earlier form of Danish (Old Danish), and it is the Norwegians who settled in the north-west. (Beware: some commentators use the term Old Norse as a blanket term for earlier

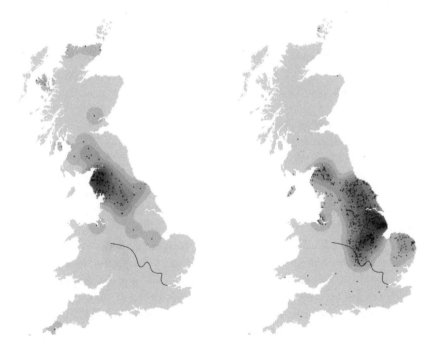

Map 1.2
Placename
evidence:
Norwegian (left)
and Danish (right)

forms of Norwegian *and* Danish.) Placename evidence has been used to account for the movements and settlement of peoples, as I have done above. But caution is needed. Just because a location has a particular placename does not necessarily mean that it was 'settled' by, say, Scandinavians. It is possible, for example, that a placename was changed by a Scandinavian official, but that few Scandinavians actually settled in that location.

As with Anglo-Saxon placenames, a number of Scandinavian place-names were formed by adding the name of the tribal leader (e.g. *Corby* = Kori's village; *Formby* = Forni's village). In some cases, an Anglo-Saxon tribal leader's name was simply replaced by a Scandinavian one. Sometimes this led to a situation where within one placename there was a word of Scandinavian origin as well as one of Anglo-Saxon origin. The classic – though disputed – example is *Grimston*, which was thought to combine the Scandinavian personal name *Grímr* with the Anglo-Saxon word *tun* (= village). Other examples are *Rolston* and *Oulston*, whose first elements are formed from the Scandinavian names *Hróllfr* and *Ulfr*.

Hybrid forms Words of mixed origin are called HYBRID FORMS.

The fourth wave of newcomers were the Norman French, who invaded England in 1066. Norman French became a prestige language spoken by the upper ranks and used for administration. Most traditional place-names, however, were left unchanged, perhaps so that administration could continue smoothly. Amazingly, a Norman force of about 10,000 had captured a country whose inhabitants are thought to number about 1 million (estimates of population are especially controversial). Clearly, the numbers would only allow the replacement of people in key positions with Normans. But some placenames were changed. As with Anglo-Saxon and Scandinavian placenames, sometimes the personal name of the local lord of the manor or powerful family became part of the placename. For example:

> Melton *Mowbray* (Roger de Moubray)
> Leighton *Buzzard* (the Busard family)
> Stanstead *Mountfitchet* (the Montifiquet family)

However, note that French personal names often stand alone, usually as the second word in a placename. French, unlike some of the other languages we have considered, did not greatly interfere with the traditional placename. In some cases, as happened with Scandinavian-influenced names, the pronunciation was slightly changed so that it would be easier for a French speaker. For example, Nottingham originally had the (perhaps less attractive from the point of view of today!) name *Snotingeham*. The first two sounds are an unusual combination for a French speaker, so the [s] was dropped. Possibly the most common

French words to be incorporated into placenames are *beau* and *bel*, which mean beautiful or fine (e.g. *Beaulieu* = beautiful place; *Beaumont* = beautiful mountain; *Belvoir* = beautiful view). These positive terms were sometimes used to improve the image suggested by a placename, as when *Fulanpetta* ('foul pit') was changed to *Beaumont*.

What about more recent developments in placenames? In Britain, very few placenames have been coined in recent centuries. According to one source, about 98 per cent of current English placenames originated before 1500. The few placenames that have been recently created tend to commemorate famous events and people. For example:

> *Battles*: Waterloo, Maida Vale, Peacehaven
> *People*: Nelson, Telford, Peterlee

An interesting modern development is the transference of a placename from one country to another. For plentiful examples of placename transference it is best to look outside Britain and in particular at areas of the world that were subjected to British colonisation. In the United States, for instance, we find the transferred British placenames *Birmingham, Bristol, Cambridge, Canterbury, Lancaster, New Castle, Norwich, Swansea* and many others. However, it is not the case that British colonisers could operate in total isolation from the local population. In many cases local placenames survived, despite the colonisers' attempts to create a second England by transferring placenames out of Britain. As a result, in former British colonies one typically finds a mixture of transferred British placenames and native placenames. To some extent, the same is true of the English spoken by the colonisers: it came into contact with the local language and adopted some of its particular characteristics, leading to a distinct variety of English. This globalisation of English is an important development and we shall return to it in Unit 11.

EXERCISES

1.2 If you live in Britain, investigate the placenames of your area. If you do not live in Britain, use a fairly detailed map of Britain and select a particular area. Take at least 15 placenames and use the readings suggested at the end of this unit to discover how those placenames came about. Classify your placenames according to (a) the period in which they were devised; (b) etymology, i.e. Celtic, Latin, Anglo-Saxon, Scandinavian, French; (c) the kind of element involved (e.g. personal name, description of local landscape or vegetation, commemorative);

and (d) the form of the placename (e.g. a single word, a compound, a hybrid). Try to relate any trends you discover to historical or cultural factors.

1.3 To what extent did British colonisers use transferred British placenames?

(a) Investigate the placenames of Australia. You could just consider the most important placenames in Australia, or, with a more detailed map, the placenames of a particular state.

(b) Investigate the placenames of the United States. You could make the study more interesting by comparing three states: one from the east, one from the south and one from the west. Make sure that you sample the same number of placenames from each state.

You will need to devise your own classification system, perhaps including such categories as transferred placenames (with sub-categories according to where the placename was transferred from, e.g. Britain, France), biographic (with subcategories according to the nationality of the person the place was named after), or language derivation (with sub-categories according to the language involved, e.g. English, French, Spanish, Aboriginal, Indian). At the conclusion of your investigation, calculate percentages for your various categories, so that you can compare the relative importance of different types of placename.

DISCUSSION POINT

Just as placenames can be revealing, so can personal names. The earliest English hereditary surnames appear shortly after the Norman Conquest. Investigate the history of your surname. Does your name seem to be associated with a particular language? Is it associated with a particular region? Is it in fact originally a placename? Is it the name of an occupation, or does it specify a particular family relationship? If you are part of a group, find out the histories of other surnames. Are there particular trends within your group?

SUMMARY

- In its history, Britain has been populated by a number of different peoples (Britons, Romans, Anglo-Saxons, Scandinavians, French) speaking different languages. This diversity has had an important effect – as we shall see during the course of this book – on the way the English language has developed.
- By investigating the etymology of placenames, we can appreciate the influence of a diverse range of languages at various points in time, and also gain insight into the social, cultural and economic history of Britain.
- Studying the history of English involves carefully weighing evidence. We must be careful not to rely on assumptions. Evidence can be of varying types – this chapter drew upon archaeological evidence, for example – but it should not be taken at face value. Historical change in spelling, for example, can easily disguise the etymology of a word.

FOLLOW-UP READING AND RESEARCH

The key pages on placenames in David Crystal's *Encyclopedia of the English Language* (Cambridge: Cambridge University Press, 2003) are pp. 140–7. For a discussion of personal names see pp. 148–53. Good introductory books on placenames are Kenneth Cameron's *English Place-Names* (London: Batsford, 1996) and Margaret Gelling's *Signposts to the Past: English Placenames and the History of England* (London: Phillimore, 2000). Eilert Ekwall's *The Concise Oxford Dictionary of English Place-Names* (Oxford: Clarendon Press, 1960) is a valuable source of information, as is Victor Watts's *Cambridge Dictionary of English Place-names* (Cambridge: Cambridge University Press, 2004). For American placenames a standard source of information is George R. Stewart's *A Concise Dictionary of American Place-Names* (New York: Oxford University Press, 1970). A good introductory book on surnames is P.H. Reaney's *The Origin of English Surnames* (London: Routledge, 1967). For reference purposes, a decent work is Patrick Hanks and Flavia Hodges' *A Dictionary of Surnames* (Oxford: Oxford University Press, 1988). This unit has tapped into a lot of British history. Now might be the time to brush yours up! An excellent survey of the main period we have been dealing with in this unit is Edward James's *Britain in the First Millennium* (London: Arnold, 2001). Alternatively, explore the websites given in Appendix VI for general British history.

2 INVESTIGATING CHANGE IN ENGLISH

English is constantly changing, and all parts of the language have been affected. These changes have occurred for a variety of reasons.

Imagine that you have stomach ache and you go to the doctor. The doctor would ask you to describe your symptoms – you groan, clutch your stomach – and also to describe the relevant background to your symptoms. You would probably be asked such questions as: When did the trouble start? Have you eaten anything that might have caused it? Has it affected your appetite? By investigating the medical history relevant to your present state, the doctor can learn more about your stomach ache. I say relevant because obviously a doctor would not ask you such a question as: Has your big toe been hurting? The case with language is similar. By investigating the history that is relevant to the present state of the English language, we can gain insight into that language, and we can begin to explain how it got to be as it is. For example, we can explain why it is that we have such apparently crazy spelling; how it is that words come into existence; why it is that sometimes we seem to have a choice of words to express more or less the same thing (e.g. *fortunate* and *lucky*); where the confusing apostrophe-*s* (e.g. *student*'s or *students*') came from; why it is that we don't all talk like the queen or the people on the BBC; and so on. By looking at how English has changed, and the factors that have influenced those changes, we can begin to answer questions like these.

However, accounting for changes in English is not straightforward. No complete historical account is without controversy, just as a newspaper report of a car crash might contain relatively uncontroversial 'facts' (e.g. how many vehicles were involved), and relatively controversial 'facts' (e.g. the cause of the crash was due to a tyre blow-out). The first type of fact relates to what happened, the second to why it happened. What happened in the history of English is becoming relatively well understood, though there is still much research to be done. Why English changed the way it did and the implications of those changes are much more disputable, because they are less observable. Just as the crash-scene investigator infers causes from observable evidence, so must the linguist. In doing so, the investigator/linguist refers to or develops theories; in other words, an account that will not only explain what happened in one set of set of data, but might predict what will happen in another. For example, the observable weakening of a tyre-wall may lead one to predict that a blow-out will happen; or, the observable weakening (disappearance) of grammatical endings on words may lead one to predict that grammatical functions will be achieved in other ways (e.g. through word-order changes) (we will consider this particular change in Units 7 and 8).

Where language differs from the tyre-walls and crashes is in the fact that it is considerably more complex. Because of this, total predictability is unrealistic: a weakened tyre-wall will eventually lead to a blow-out at high speed; with language, sometimes a change simply stops. For instance, at one point it looked as if the word *wising* was going to enter English vocabulary. This word came about when a certain vacuum cleaner company made a mess of their free holiday offer. They did not have enough money to pay for the vast number of people who applied for a holiday, so they tried to put off the applicants by making the holiday dates and airport destinations as inconvenient as possible. This 'putting off' technique was called *wising* after the manager who directed it. Words are often added to English, in order to represent areas of meaning that need representing. This 'putting off' technique is still regularly used today, so, theoretically, it needs representation by a word – thus one might predict that *wising* is alive and well. But, for some reason, *wising* has fizzled out. More accurately, then, linguists typically aim at producing elegant and parsimonious accounts of language changes they know to have occurred; they are not, like crash investigators trying to prevent future crashes, in the business of predicting what will occur. In the coming paragraphs, we will first comment broadly on the fact that changes in English have occurred, then we will look more closely at what has changed and finally we will consider some possible reasons as to why it has changed.

The fact that English has changed is plain to see. Look at Text 1 in Appendix IV, written in the ninth century. It looks alien, and it is difficult to read without special training. Compare this with Text 2, written by a contemporary of Chaucer in 1387. It is usually possible to get the gist of Chaucer without the aid of a dictionary. Shakespeare seems to be much more familiar waters, although it is not all plain sailing. Text 5 was written three years after Shakespeare was born. When we reach the middle of the seventeenth century, and more particularly the eighteenth century, our problems seem reduced to the occasional word. Text 7 was written in 1644. And finally with the twentieth century, we may feel that we have reached home ground. However, just because the English language becomes more comprehensible as it nears our present day, it does not in any way mean that the language has stopped changing. Consider a couple of recent changes. The word *funny* is increasingly being used as a noun; in other words, not 'he's a funny man', where it is an adjective, but 'he told a funny', meaning he said something humorous. The word *carjacking* (sometimes written with a space between the two words instead of the hyphen), the act of illegally commandeering and stealing somebody's car, is a new word, modelled on 'hijacking'. (Interestingly, *carjacking* is not yet written as a solid word, as 'hijacking' is.) The general point I'm making is that all living languages are in a state of change.

The texts I referred to above fall within different periods in the development of the English language, and, traditionally, scholars have defined and labelled these periods in particular ways. Text 1 falls within the period known as OLD ENGLISH (OE), running from about AD 450 to 1100. Chaucer, along with Text 2, falls within the MIDDLE ENGLISH (ME) period, approximately spanning the years 1100–1500. It may come as a surprise to some of you to learn that Shakespeare, along with Texts 5, 6 and 7, is usually considered part of MODERN ENGLISH (Mod.E), which runs from 1500 to the present day. However, Modern English is often subdivided: EARLY MODERN ENGLISH (EMod.E) spans the years 1500 to about 1750, and LATE MODERN ENGLISH (LMod.E) spans the remaining years. Of course, these are conventional labels for these periods. In fact, you will find that different scholars often put the boundaries in slightly different places. Certainly, it is not the case that somebody apparently speaking Middle English in 1499 suddenly started speaking Modern English in 1501. This scenario would imply that the language didn't change within these periods, but then underwent a cataclysmic change when it reached a boundary. Nevertheless, while some caution is needed, these terms are convenient labels for these periods, which, very broadly speaking, correlate with major linguistic changes, as well as major cultural, social and political changes. Consider, for example, these historical events. Old English is often dated from the arrival of Anglo-Saxon settlers in 449 (though others date it from 700, the point from which decent quantities of written English survive). The Norman Conquest in 1066 is obviously important in defining the beginning of Middle English (though some push the date to 1250, on the basis that the effect of the Norman Conquest on the English language was not immediate). William Caxton's introduction of the printing press in about 1476 is an important factor in suggesting the beginning of Modern English: printing helped promote a national standard for written English, as we shall see in Unit 13. Of course, these periods are characterised by more factors than this. You will discover more about the linguistic changes that took place during these periods in the following units.

Old English (OE)

Middle English (ME)

Modern English (Mod.E)

Early modern English (EMod.E)

Late modern English (LMod.E)

What has changed in the English language? It is possible to find changes at every level of language, as demonstrated in Exercise 2.1.

EXERCISES

2.1 Have a close look at Text 1 in Appendix IV, an OE text from the ninth-century *Anglo-Saxon Chronicle*. My word-for-word translation does not reflect what we would naturally do in contemporary English; it sounds awkward. So, write a fluent, easy-to-read version (in particular, this will require changing the order of words, adding words and changing the punctuation).

Now, look back through all the different versions and consider how they have changed. (This is rather like a spot-the-difference competition.) Note down as many of the linguistic changes as you can, using the grid below. In the left-hand column of the grid you will find that language has been broken down into different levels. More technical names for these levels are given in parentheses. To the right of this column I have suggested a series of questions you can ask yourself – questions that should help you to decide what features of Text 1 to place under a particular linguistic level. The right-hand column is for your examples (of course, you can always expand this on a separate piece of paper). You will experience difficulty with one linguistic level – 'sound'. Clearly, you cannot hear Text 1. I shall discuss 'sound' in the following unit. I suggest you leave this level blank for now. If you are interested in finding out what OE might have sounded like, browse through the recordings at: www.georgetown.edu/faculty/ballc/O.E./O.E.-audio.html (does the pronunciation remind you of any modern languages?). In general, the main aim of this task is that you should gain some experience in identifying linguistic features at different levels. Don't worry if you cannot find a comprehensive list of features for every level from Text 1. In the following units we will be focusing on each of these linguistic levels and on many more example texts.

Linguistic Level	Questions to ask yourself	Examples from Text 1
Writing (Graphetics/ Graphology)	Are unfamiliar letters, spellings and punctuation marks used? What words are capitalised?	

Sound (Phonetics/ Phonology)	How are words pronounced? Are there unfamiliar speech sounds?
Structure (Grammar: morphology/ syntax)	Are there unfamiliar endings on words? In your contemporary version have you had to supply extra words not present in the original? Have words been placed in an unfamiliar order?
Words (Lexis)	Are there unfamiliar words?
Meaning (Semantics)	Are there words used with unfamiliar meanings?

2.2 What strikes you as new and fashionable in English today? Write down as many examples as you can. Now consider to what linguistic level these innovations belong. Do this before reading the 'answer' in Appendix V.

Exercise 2.1 looks in depth at one text. Appendix IV, the 'mini-corpus' of texts, is organised chronologically, giving a few snapshots of English moving from OE to the present day. A note of caution needs to be sounded about comparing two different texts written at two different points in time. We need to make sure that we compare like with like, or, if this is not possible, we need to be aware of any potential distortion in our observations. Comparing, for example, a religious text with a speech would be hazardous, since religious texts often contain archaisms, whereas spoken language often contains novelties. Thus, a comparison of Text 3 (a letter written in haste) or Text 5 (a popular literary text containing dialogue) with, say, Text 1 (a formal historical record) or Text 6 (extracts from the Bible) would need to be conducted with some caution.

Why does English change, or, indeed, languages in general? Here are some possible reasons:

1   Some changes within the language have come about largely as a result of the fact that language operates, at least to some extent, as a **Structural system** STRUCTURAL SYSTEM. For example, the linguistic levels, as seen in Exercise 2.1, are interconnected – change in one part can cause change in another. To take a simple example, during the Renaissance, scholars, influenced by Latin and Greek, decided to add *h* to a number of words. Thus, although in ME the word for 'throne' was spelt *trone*, scholars added an *h*, because the Latin word was spelt *thronus* (where the 'th' was a rendering of 'theta', the first letter of

the Greek word, θϱόνος). This resulted in the first sound of the word being pronounced differently, [θ] instead of [t]. [*Stop!* You have just encountered symbols designed to represent speech sounds. Turn to Appendix III and read the short explanation there.] A similar change occurred in the words *Katherine* (modelled on the Greek word meaning 'pure'), and *theatre* and *anthem*, though perhaps for different reasons. So, a change in graphology – a change in spelling – led to a change in pronunciation. Note, however, that this was not a regular change – it did not happen in all cases. Not every spelling <t> was respelt <th>. Moreover, in one notable case, the name *Anthony*, the respelling took place, but the change in pronunciation did not. REGULARITY is an important issue in language change.

Regularity

2　Think of a situation where two languages are spoken within the same country or community. The languages are brought into close contact, and some members of the community will speak more than one language and frequently switch between languages. This language or 'code switching' will lead to the mutual influence of those languages. LANGUAGE CONTACT is an important factor in the history of English when you bear in mind the invasions and settlement of Britain by peoples speaking diverse languages – Celtic languages, Germanic dialects and French.

Language contact

3　When considering the effect of other languages on English, SPEAKERS' ATTITUDES need to be taken into consideration. French was (and perhaps still is) a high-prestige language for the English, as were the classical languages, Greek and Latin. Thus people copied these languages for social reasons, perhaps to sound more sophisticated or cultivated. The reverse is also true. For example, for the Germans, French has not been a high-prestige language as in Britain, and as a result has had relatively little effect on German, despite the fact that Germany is adjacent to France.

Speakers' attitudes

4　The changes that have occurred in our physical environment, our culture, our social structures, our social attitudes and so on are often reflected in language, particularly in vocabulary and meaning. Consider the following examples of relatively new words and (in parentheses) the developments they reflect: *euro-sceptic* (political), *politically correct* (social attitudes), *user friendly* (technological), and many words for Italian cooking, such as *pesto*, *balsamic* vinegar, *fusilli* (cultural).

The final point I want to make in this unit is perhaps the most important – it is something I want you to do. I want you, during the course of this book, to reassess the FOLK BELIEFS you have about language, and particularly about language change. We all have such

Folk beliefs

beliefs – they are a part of the fabric of social life. But we need to see them for what they are and not be blinded by them. A key folk belief is that 'written language is best'. This is key, because it underlies lots of other beliefs, for example: 'good pronunciation follows writing', 'good grammar follows writing', 'children should be taught the grammar of writing' and 'variation is bad'. It is also a factor underlying the belief 'change is bad' (writing is relatively permanent compared with speech). It is possible to challenge all of these beliefs, and I will return to some of them in future units. Here, I will examine one sentence written by a student of mine at the beginning of the course:

> It is a fact that in the 20th century the working-class were completely illiterate and communicated with each other in a very simplistic manner not recognisable as speech.

The logic seems to be: 'In the past the working-class were uneducated and therefore illiterate. Literacy enables you to communicate in speech, and therefore without it you can only grunt.' Let's take this apart. First, before 1870 and the Education Act, most of the 'working class' were uneducated. At the time of writing, the twentieth century is only four years ago, so it is not the case that the working class were 'completely illiterate' then. Second, literacy does not correlate with speech in the way many people believe. Everybody – upper-class folk included – would reduce a form like *and* in a phrase like 'fish n chips'.

EXERCISE

2.3   Get hold of a recording of the Queen (or a member of the royal family). Find a segment where she uses 'and' a lot. Now listen to each case very carefully. What does she actually say?

In fact, it is the 'working-classes' *and* the 'upper-classes' that have tended to 'drop' sounds like the [h] of *hospital*. Higher levels of literacy have correlated with the 'middle-classes', who, being more aware of the spelling, have tended to adapt to it. Third, literacy cannot be the sole basis of 'speech'. In the evolution of language, speech comes before writing. Moreover, many languages have no writing systems at all, but have a spoken language capable of many functions, including oral literature. Remember that English itself in earlier centuries was for the mass of the population a purely spoken language.

Folk beliefs are often a launch pad for a PRESCRIPTIVE APPROACH to language: the idea that one variety or feature of language has an inherently higher value than others. Symptomatic of this approach is judgemental (and frequently emotional) language: 'good', 'bad', 'simplistic', 'sloppy', 'lazy', 'careless', 'decay', 'impoverish', etc. What about 'illiterate'? It too conveys a negative value judgement. Value is determined by beliefs about what counts as prestigious (e.g. writing, Latin) and how language works (e.g. following the principles of logic). Certain varieties/features are 'prescribed' (i.e. to be followed), others are 'proscribed' (i.e. to be avoided), and all this is typically, couched as lists of 'dos' and 'don'ts'. Linguists generally claim to take a DESCRIPTIVE APPROACH: the idea that the task of linguists is to 'describe' the facts, based on observation, experimentation and argument.

Prescriptive approach

Descriptive approach

EXERCISE

2.4 Where would you put the stress in the words below – on the first syllable or the second?

applicable, comparable, controversy, lamentable

Test these words on a group of young people, and then compare your results with a group of much older people. If you have discovered trends among the two groups and those trends differ, can you now identify a general shift in the stress of polysyllabic words like these – an example of language change in progress? Of course, one can only guess that such a change will be completed: as we noted above, a language change can always fizzle out or even be reversed.

DISCUSSION POINT

One influence on change in English has been the rules or ideas devised by people in authority. People often try to do what they think they should be doing. Rules have prestige. For example, my junior-school teacher told me never to begin a sentence with the word *and*, and, as a consequence, I tend not to. In fact, it only takes a quick look through the *OED* entry on *and* to realise that beginning a sentence with *and* is a useful way of conveying a number of particular meanings, and that it has a well-established history. Now, write down some of the prescriptive rules or ideas that influence your language usage. If you are part of a group, gather up people's lists, and draw up a list of the most frequently mentioned rules. In this way, you should gain some insight into what the most popular 'dos' and 'don'ts' are. Discuss the following questions: Are all linguistic levels covered? Do people really follow all these rules? Do the rules apply equally, and are they followed equally in speech and writing? If not, what does this suggest about differences in change in speech and writing? Is any rationale given for these rules?

SUMMARY

- English, in common with all living languages, is in a continual state of change.
- Change is not fully predictable.
- Change occurs at all levels of the language, though it is not equally observable. Relatively rapid changes in vocabulary are easily observed; relatively slower changes in grammar are less easily observed.
- Change in one part of the language system can lead to changes in other parts of the system. Changes may vary in terms of how regular they are (i.e. do they apply to the whole set of relevant items or only part of the set?).
- Change is likely to occur when languages are mixed.
- Speakers are likely to imitate prestige languages and this can lead to change. They also may attempt to follow prescriptive rules, partly because of their prestige.
- Language change can reflect changes in the physical environment, culture, social structure, social attitudes, etc.

FOLLOW-UP READING

Accessible overviews of the development of English are given in Robert Burchfield's *The English Language* (Oxford: Oxford University Press, 2002) and David Crystal's *The English Language: A Guided Tour of the Language* (2nd edn, London: Pelican, 2002). For an introductory book on linguistic change in general, try Jean Aitchison's *Language Change: Progress or Decay* (3rd edn, Cambridge: Cambridge University Press, 2001), or Larry Trask's more advanced *Historical Linguistics* (London: Arnold, 1996). For more on folk beliefs and myths about language, I recommend Laurie Bauer's and Peter Trudgill's *Language Myths* (London: Penguin Books, 1998), an illuminating and readable collection of short essays written by expert linguists.

SPELLINGS AND SPEECH SOUNDS

3

English spelling used to represent speech sounds in a relatively simple way, but a variety of changes have led to a much more complex system.

Does spelling represent the pronunciation of words? The answer to that question is a rather important one, since, if it does, then learning to spell is quite straightforward.

EXERCISE

3.1   In the minds of some educationalists it clearly does. Minette Marrin, writing in the *Sunday Times* newspaper, like many other impassioned commentators, argues for 'old-fashioned' 'phonics' (i.e. speech sounds). Spelling, apparently, is simply a matter of matching letters and sounds, as in 'C-A-T'. How true is this? Take the word *cat* as your test-case. How many different sounds can each letter represent?

Let's compare English spelling with Italian. The word for *enough* in Italian is *basta*. The letters of *basta* represent the sounds of the spoken word (pronounced like *pasta*, except for the opening sound). Generally when these sounds occur in other words they are represented by the same letters. Now consider *enough*. Clearly, the spelling does not represent the units of sound that make up the spoken word in a straightforward way. When these sounds occur in other words, they can be represented by other letters. In each of the pairs below, the emboldened letters represent the same sound:

en**ough**   **a**nnounce
en**ou**gh   m**u**ch
enou**gh**   **f**at

Phonemic   Unlike Italian, English spelling is not always PHONEMIC. There is no simple one-to-one correspondence between phonemes – the smallest units of speech distinguishing one word from another – and the letters that represent them. (Not surprisingly, in Italy literacy is not the problem that it is in England, since you more or less write down what you say.) In contrast with today, spelling in the OE period was rather more phonemic. Generally, OE spelling does not contain 'silent letters'. For example, consider the words *twa* ('two') and *lang* ('long') given in Text 1 (Appendix IV). The <w> of *twa* was originally pronounced, and thus, unlike today, each letter of the spelling corresponded to a phoneme of the spoken word. Similarly, the final <g> of *lang* was pronounced, so that the pronunciation of the word would be [lɒng]. Indeed, the final <g> of this word and of others (e.g. *tongue*, *ring*) is still pronounced in some west-central areas of England. (Listen to some of the recordings at: http://www.bbc.co.uk/voices/. This feature is particularly clear in the Liverpool recordings.)

Why has the spelling system become less phonemic? Why is it now so complicated? History, as we shall see, can provide an explanation. Initially, English was written in a Germanic alphabet – the Runic alphabet. Only a few Runic English texts survive, such as the inscriptions on the Ruthwell Cross, thought to date back to AD 700. (Images of the cross, its inscriptions and information about the Runic alphabet, can be found at: http://www.flsouthern.edu/eng/abruce/rood/IMAGES.HTM.) Christian missionaries, arriving in Britain in 597 spreading literacy, used forms of the 23-letter Roman alphabet: A B C D E F G H I K L M N O P Q R S T V X Y Z. And this is the first problem for English spelling: it adopted the Roman alphabet, in other words, the alphabet of another language – Latin. Today, we have over 40 phonemes in English, but only 26 letters by which to represent those phonemes. In particular, note that we have about 20 vowel sounds in English, but only 5 vowel letters (Exercise 3.1 illustrated the particular problem with vowels). Even in OE the Latin alphabet on its own was not enough; some sounds had no letter counterpart (the first two items appear in Text 1):

•   [w], the first sound of *wet*, was written with a runic symbol <ƿ> (called 'wynn'). Later replaced by northern French <uu> or <w>; it was rare after 1300.

- [θ] and [ð], as in the first sounds of *thin* and *the*, were represented by a runic symbol <þ> (called 'thorn', sometimes written without the cross-bar), and later by <ð> (called 'eth'), which was possibly an Irish development of Latin <d>. Both were used interchangeably, and then in ME begin to be replaced by <th>.

- [æ], the vowel of *mat*, was represented by two 'ligatured' Latin letters <a> and <e> to form <æ> (called 'ash', after a runic symbol that represented the same sound). It stopped being used in the ME period.

The ME <th>, referred to above, is an example of a DIGRAPH, where one phoneme is represented by a pair of letters. Note that digraphs by definition represent a move away from simple 'one phoneme = one letter' correspondences. OE <æ> could be seen as a kind of digraph, and there were others in this period: <sc> was usually used to represent the phoneme [ʃ], as in the first sound of the OE word *scep* and its present-day counterpart 'sheep'; <cg> was usually used to represent the phoneme [dʒ], as in the last sound of the OE word *ecg* and its present day counterpart 'edge'. Also, the digraphs <ea> and <eo> were used in OE, as in the words *eare* 'ear' and *beor* 'beer'. (Examples of some of these letters can be found in Text 1.)

Digraph

EXERCISES

3.2 It should be remembered that in OE and ME there were no firm conventions for spelling. Greater variation was tolerated than would be today. In particular, a writer's spelling would tend to reflect whatever dialect they happened to speak. (We will consider this further in Unit 9.) The *OED* lists the variant spellings of words. To get an idea of the degree of spelling variation, check the spellings of the following words: *spear*, *sword* and *shield*.

3.3 Given that spelling used to represent much more closely the pronunciation of words, what can you infer about changes in the pronunciation of the following words? Consider the letters that do not correspond to any of the sounds in your own pronunciation of these words. The lack of correspondence between spelling and pronunciation reflects pronunciation changes that have occurred over the centuries. Were those changes regular? Did they just occur in the context of certain sounds? For example, in *walk*, *half* and *folk* we do not pronounce the <l>, but we do in *milk*.

sword
walk, half, folk
wreck, write, wring
gnat, gnarl, gnaw
knee, know, knight

Exercise 3.3 examines words that still have the traces of earlier pronunciations in their spellings. Some word spellings have left no trace. Consider OE *hnutu* 'nut', *hring* 'ring' and *hlaford* 'lord'. English used to permit word-initial <h> before <n>, <r> and <l> (I will comment on <h> before <w> separately below). It is thought that <h> in such contexts was pronounced [x], as in the last sound of Scottish *loch*. It ceased to be pronounced by early ME, and this timing explains why the spelling changed here and not in the example sets *walk*, *wreck*, *gnat* and *knee* above. The latter pronunciation changes only got under way in late ME/ EMod.E at the time when the spelling system was becoming fixed – spelling did not keep up with pronunciation changes. The letter <h>, pronounced either [x] as in OE or [h] as now, is generally susceptible to loss. It requires minimal effort to make these sounds – basically just restricting the airflow in your throat (more precisely, for the terminology fans, [x] is a velar fricative and [h] a glottal fricative). Doing less than [h] leads to nothing. 'Doing less' is in fact a reason for some pronunciation changes: people regularly make changes so that words can be said with less effort. Let me illustrate this by broadening the perspective. If we trace the OE words *hnutu* and *hring* back to Indo-European (refresh your memory of Appendix II), the word-forms were thought to be 'knud' and 'krengho'. Observe that there was originally <k> instead of <h>. Make the sounds [k] and [h] – [k] requires more muscular effort and the result is a punchier sound. The change to a 'weaker' consonant, one that requires less effort and is more vowel-like, involves a process called

Lenition LENITION. Quite a number of English words now pronounced with initial [h] originally had [k]. Evidence of this can be found in comparing English words with languages that have preserved the [k]. Consider the following English–Italian pairs: 'head–capo', 'hill–collina', 'heat–caldo', and 'heart–cuore'. In fact, the English forms have weakened further than this suggests: except for a few regional accents, 'dropping' the initial [h] is a regular feature for all types of speaker (even the Queen does it for some words!). Note the implications of this paragraph: the prescriptivists howl about 'h-dropping', but it is part of a normal process of weakening that has been taking place over thousands of years.

EXERCISE

3.4 This is partly a listening exercise. Listen to some of the Liverpool recordings at: http://www.bbc.co.uk/voices/. How do some speakers pronounce the final consonant in words like *back*? Is this part of a regular process of change?

A number of the apparent oddities of English spelling were introduced by ME scribes, particularly Norman scribes who adapted spelling to suit French spelling conventions. Digraphs promoted by ME scribes include:

- <sh> replacing <sc> in words like OE *scip* 'ship'.
- <gh> replacing <h> in words like OE *riht* 'right'.
- <ch> replacing <c> in words like OE *cin* 'chin'.
- <wh> replacing <hw> in words like OE *hwæt* 'what' (an inadequate translation of a versatile item).
- <qu> replacing <cw> in words like OE *cwen* 'queen'. (Note that *cw* was in fact a much more obvious English representation of the first sounds of words like *queen*.)
- <ou> (or <ow>) replacing <u> in words like OE *hus* 'house' and *nu* 'now'. (Consider the pronunciation of *ou* in French words such as *vous*.)

Note the role of <h> in the first three items (and also in <th> mentioned earlier) – <h> is doing the job that DIACRITICS do in some other languages. Diacritics are the marks added to letters to alter the pronunciation (e.g. à, á, â, ã, ä, å). For example, one of my colleagues has a Czech husband whose name is Ivanic, except that is how English people often misspell it: it should be Ivanič. To achieve the right pronunciation in English spelling, one would have to write 'Ivanich'. The letter <h> in <wh> is different from the previous cases, since it came about as a re-ordering of <hw>. This was an unfortunate change, since people used to pronounce the <h> before the <w>. In fact, some speakers – some Scottish speakers, for example – still do pronounce something like an [h] before the [w], making a distinction between words like *wear* and words like *where*.

The lettter <c> had originally represented two sounds: the first sounds of the words *chin* (OE *cin*) and *king* (OE *cyning*), i.e. [tʃ] and [k]. With the development of the diagraph <ch>, <ch> could be used to distinguish [tʃ] from [k], which could be represented by <c>. So, does <c> now straightforwardly represent one sound, [k]? If this were the case,

Diacritics

we would be replicating the ancient convention whereby the Roman alphabet represented an aspect of Latin; thus, the first syllable of the Latin word *centrum* (meaning 'centre') was pronounced as we would say the name *Ken*. In fact, some OE words, such as *cuman* 'come' or *cu* 'cow', have survived into present day English with <c> representing [k], and some Latin-derived words – *common, replicate, act*, and so on – maintain the original Roman convention in English. However, English borrowed French vocabulary, where the value of <c> is often [s] (e.g. *centre, face, difference*), and English went further with this convention, using <c> for [s] in words like OE *is* 'ice'. The result is that the letter <c> represents more than one sound, and for that reason has been a favourite target of spelling reformers, who argue that [k] should be generally assigned to <k> (as, for example, is usually the case in Modern German). The culprit in all this is our friend lenition, coupled with the borrowing of words. The [k] of *centrum* had weakened in French to the [s] of *centre*. Interestingly, Modern Italian has not weakened as far as French: it has *centro*, where the first sound is [tʃ], as in the first sound of *ciao*. Say the three sounds – Latin [k], Modern Italian [tʃ], and French [s] – in order to get a sense of the weakening sound (you will also find that where you make the sound with your tongue changes).

The adoption of <ou> helped to indicate a long vowel without having to use double <u>. The problem with double <u> was legibility. The characters <u, uu, i, n, m> were all written with straight down-strokes or 'minims' and were thus in danger of being confused. In fact, to make things clearer, scribes sometimes wrote <o> for <u> and <y> for <i>. Thus, the word *come* was once spelt '𝔱𝔲𝔪𝔢' (= 'cume'), a spelling that was closer to pronunciation but not so legible. Similar changes were made to, for example, *love, son* and *wolf*.

Standardisation   The advent of printing with William Caxton in 1476 was a step towards the STANDARDISATION of spellings. Printing was most economic if one set of spelling conventions reflecting one dialect was chosen. We shall consider the choice of dialect Caxton made in Unit 10. For now, let's note that printing made possible the production of a vast amount of reading material using one set of spelling conventions: it could promote a 'standard' in spelling. This is not to suggest that the early printers entirely agreed on what the standard should be or were consistent in applying it. In some respects the printers added to the oddities of spelling. Many of the early printers were Dutch, and sometimes Dutch spellings influenced English words. For example, the word *ghost* in OE was spelt *gast*, but the Dutch printers added an <h>, presumably influenced by the Flemish word *gheest*. Furthermore, the Dutch printers used continental characters. Thus non-Latin letters, such as 'thorn'<þ>, were not well represented. In fact, a <y> was chosen to represent 'thorn'. A remnant of this can be seen in the sign *Ye Olde Tea Shoppe*, where *Ye* is equivalent to *The* (remember: thorn was replaced with <th>). This sign also illustrates other characteristics of EMod.E spelling, which printers were at least partly responsible for. Printers often added a superfluous <e> (e.g. *Olde*), doubled up consonants (e.g. *Shoppe*), or used <y> instead of <i> because they took up more space. This was done in order to increase the length of a line so that it would match the others. All this added to the general variability in spelling. Line justification today, as in the very text I am writing now, is automatically achieved on a word processor without varying the spelling.

EXERCISE

3.5 Study the spelling in Texts 3 and 4 (Appendix IV). What inconsistencies in the spelling can you find? Can you explain why some of these occur? Consider the use of the letters *v* and *u*. At this time a *v* could be used for a *u* and vice versa, but they were not completely interchangeable. What determines the use of one letter or the other? The letters *i* and *y* are sometimes said to be interchangeable. How true is this?

In the sixteenth century, there was particular interest in the classical languages Latin and Greek, and these had much prestige. It was fashionable to respell words in order to make them look more like the originals, although this meant adding silent letters. These ETYMOLOGICAL RESPELLINGS include:

Etymological respellings

ME *langage*	>	*language* (Latin *lingua*)
ME *dette*	>	*debt* (Latin *debitum*)
ME *receite*	>	*receipt* (Latin *receptum*)
ME *samon*	>	*salmon* (Latin *salmo*)

However, sometimes the respellers got their etymology wrong. For example, it was assumed that ME *iland* came from French *isle*, and thus <s> was added to make *island*. In fact, *iland* was an OE word, and has Germanic roots. (Consult Texts 2 and 3 for the old spelling of *language*.)

In the sixteenth and seventeenth centuries, many words entered English from languages such as French (e.g. *grotesque*, *colonel*), Latin (e.g. *necessary*, *relaxation*), Greek (e.g. *chaos*, *pneumonia*), Italian (e.g. *piazza*, *piano*) and Spanish (e.g. *canoe*, *tobacco*). The important consequence is that English spelling contains the spelling conventions of other languages:

it is an amalgam of various spelling systems. This process of borrowing from other languages has continued throughout the development of English. More recently, the spelling of the word *khaki* – the colour – reflects the fact that it is borrowed from Urdu, and the spelling of *kamikaze* reflects the fact that it is borrowed from Japanese.

Many people in the sixteenth century were highly critical of the tremendous variation in spelling, the addition of superfluous letters and so on. Also, from this time onwards dictionaries started to appear that people could consult for an authoritative spelling. Coupled with printing, all this had the effect of fixing or standardising spellings. In fact, very few spellings have changed since Dr Johnson's dictionary of 1755. Unfortunately, spellings were fixed at a time of great confusion. Not only was there a great influx of words from other languages, but the language was also experiencing changes in pronunciation – changes that spelling failed to keep up with. We have already seen in Exercise 3.3 how certain consonants ceased to be pronounced. Even more dramatic changes occurred in the pronun-

Great Vowel Shift (GVS)

ciation of long vowels, the so-called GREAT VOWEL SHIFT (GVS) (fondly referred to by my students as the 'Great Bowel Shift'). (Check you are familiar with the term 'long vowels'. Look at the vowels in Appendix III. A following colon marks out the long vowels.) These changes can account for why the relationship between spelling and pronunciation in words like *make*, *sweet*, *ride*, *stone* and *house* is not as simple as it once was, and so we need to look at it further. They are also relevant to explaining the diversity in English accents, something we will consider in Unit 9.

What was the GVS? Trying to tell people about sounds on paper is tricky at the best of times, but is made even more difficult when your readers would never have heard all of the sounds I am talking about. Now, however, with the rise of computers and the internet, I am considerably aided by a wonderful website devoted to the GVS. This was created primarily by Melinda Menzer, with assistance from Andrea Bean, of Furman University, and is available at: http://alpha.furman.edu/~ mmenzer/gvs/. Here, you will be able to hear what went on. The GVS refers to a set of changes whereby the pronunciation of long vowels was 'raised', and which mostly occurred between 1400 and 1650. Raising means raising the tongue towards the roof of the mouth. To get a sense of this, try saying: *bad*, *bed*, *bead* and *bard*, *bore*, *boo* (lengthen the vowels of *bad* and *bed*, to make them consistent with the others; this exercise will not work perfectly for speakers of some accents). The example below gives you a snapshot of pronunciations just before 1400 compared with those of many speakers today.

	1400		*Today?*
find	[fiːnd]	→	[faɪnd]
meet	[meːt]*	→	[miːt]

meat	[mɛːt]	→	[miːt]
name	[naːmə]*	→	[neɪm]
house	[huːs]	→	[haʊs]
goose	[goːs]*	→	[guːs]
stone	[stɔːnə]	→	[stəʊn]

I have placed a question mark against 'Today', because it is not the case that everybody has these pronunciations. Some accents did not undergo a particular change and others changed further. We will consider this briefly in Unit 9, where we look at accents and dialects. The asterisks indicate symbols – [a], [e], [o] – which are not listed in Appendix III. Again, I will have a little more to say about these in Unit 9. Here, I will give you a rough idea of these sounds (you can of course listen to them on the website opposite).

1   Speakers in the south of England and much of North America have [æ] in words like *bad*, and [ɑː] in words like *father* (though, more precisely, for North American speakers the vowel of *father* is a shorter [ɑ]). If you are from those areas, compare [æ] and [ɑː]. You will find that you use the front part of the tongue for the first and the back part for the second: the first is a front vowel and the second a back vowel. Speakers from Scotland or certain areas of northern England will not be able to compare the pronunciations of *bad* and *father* in that way, since they will use [a] for both – [a] lies roughly midway between [æː] and [ɑː]. (When speakers from southern England try to mimic the 'northern a', they usually get it wrong in using [æ].)

2   If you are from Scotland or certain areas of northern England, [eː] might be the way you pronounce the vowel of *face*, *name* and *way*. Other people, however, such as those from the south of England, are likely to have the DIPHTHONG [eɪ], which starts in the area of **Diphthong** [e] and then glides towards [ɪ]. Note that, to achieve this glide, the tongue moves slightly up; in contrast, [feːs] ('face') is said while keeping the tongue relatively still (try saying it) – it is a 'pure' MONOPHTHONG. The vowel [ɛ], as in *bed* for many speakers, is **Monophthong** said with the tongue lower than [e]. Say [ɛː] and [eː] repeatedly. (Not following all this? Trying saying 'air' and then 'ey', and you'll get the general idea.) Interestingly, our spelling system still preserves the old distinction: <ee>, as in *meet*, was generally used when the pronunciation was [eː], and <ea>, as in *meat*, when the pronunciation was [ɛː]. The loss of this distinction is one further way in which spelling has become less straightforward.

3   Similarly, [oː] is pronounced in Scotland and certain areas of northern England in words like *stone*, *road* and *goat*. For those who

do not speak with these accents, it is tricky to convey the pronunciation. Try saying *roared*, *road* and *rude*. As you move from [ɔː]
to [uː], you should find your tongue moving upwards, squeezing
the space at the back of your mouth; [oː] is in the middle position.
Remember, you want a pure monothphong here, not [əʊ]. (Not
following all this? Trying saying *rod*, but make the vowel longer.)

Phew! Now that's over, let's briefly return to that snapshot of changes
relating to the GVS given above. The changes look random, but let's map
them out like this (adapted from Boucier, G., *An Introduction to the
History of the English Language*, London: Stanley Thornes, 1981: 198):

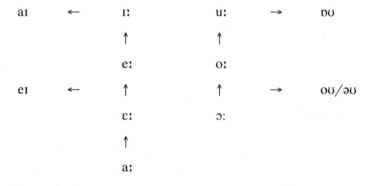

If you go back to the snapshot, you will see that the changes fit this
simplified pattern. So, the first four snapshot examples illustrate vowel
raising on the left of the diagram (front vowels), and the final three illustrate vowel raising on the right of the diagram (back vowels). For example,
vowels like that in [huːs], unable to be raised further, become for many
speakers a diphthong, [haʊs]. This doesn't mean that [uː] becomes redundant, because vowels in words like [goːs] then move up and become
[guːs]. And that doesn't mean that [oː] becomes redundant, because
vowels in words like [stɔːnə] then move up and become [stoːnə] (by
about 1600). The pronunciation of that word remains [stoːn] for some
speakers in northern England/Scotland, while it has undergone further
change for others, becoming a diphthong, [stəʊn]. An important point
Chain shift   to note is that this is all happening systematically as part of a CHAIN
SHIFT. Which bit changed first is a matter of debate. Did it start at the
top, as in my description above, and pull lower vowels up (a 'drag chain'),
or did it start at the bottom and push higher vowels further up (a 'push
chain')? Or was it both? And what caused the movement in the first place?
You can explore these questions further in the readings.

Changes in English spelling since the eighteenth century have mainly
been to do with attitudes towards the spelling system that emerged. The
old tolerance of spelling variation evaporated, and spelling came to be

seen as an indicator of education and even intelligence. In the twentieth century a number of attempts have been made to simplify spelling, the most famous campaigner for spelling reform being George Bernard Shaw. However, spelling reform has so far failed to produce any changes in British English spelling. In American English, spelling reform – promoted in particular by Noah Webster – has achieved a measure of success, leading to such spellings as *color* and *center*.

EXERCISES

3.6 In this unit we have primarily considered spelling in terms of whether there is a correspondence between phonemes – the units of speech – and the letters of words. In fact, the relationship between spelling and spoken words may be systematic, but more complex than simple one-to-one correspondence of phonemes and letters. Let's take an example. How would you pronounce the word *ghoti*? Most of us, I guess, would pronounce it in the same way as we would pronounce 'goaty'; in other words [gəʊtiː] or perhaps [goːtɪ]. Bernard Shaw coined this word to illustrate the apparent absurdities of spelling. He claimed that it should be pronounced like *fish*: <gh> as in *enough*, <o> as in *women*, and <ti> as in *nation*. But clearly spelling does not work like this; [gəʊtiː] (or [goːtɪ]) is the more obvious pronunciation of *ghoti*. Shaw fails to take into account the more complex ways in which spelling indicates pronunciation, such as by the position of letters in a word. Construct an attack on Shaw's claim. What evidence can you give to support the claim that *ghoti* should be pronounced [gəʊtiː] (or [goːtɪ]) and not as you would pronounce *fish*? (*Hint:* think of other words that begin or end with the same letters.)

3.7 (a) Many of the final <e>s on words are remnants of old grammatical endings, and were pronounced as a 'schwa' (a short vowel sound, as in the first phoneme of the word *about*). Note, for example, how I had transcribed the pronunciation of word *name* above: [naːmə]. Towards the end of the ME period the final <e> ceased to be pronounced. However, while they no longer corresponded in a simple way with single phonemes, many do provide useful information about the pronunciation of a word. Consider the words *fate*, *bite* and *mope*, with and without the final <e>. What pronunciation information does the final <e> convey? Can you find examples where this generalisation doesn't work?

(b) In OE a doubled consonant would affect the pronunciation of that consonant, as is the case in Italian today. Now this is no longer the case: <t> would be pronounced the same as <tt>. However, doubling a consonant does provide pronunciation information. Consider the following pairs of words: *sitter/seater, shutter/shooter, chatting/charting, wedding/wading*. What pronunciation information does the doubled consonant convey? Can you find examples where this generalisation doesn't work?

3.8 In one particular study, the following were found to be common misspellings: *gallary, succesful, exibition, definate, polititian, extasy, morgage.* (a) On the basis of these misspellings, describe some potential problems in English spelling. (b) Discover why these words have troublesome spellings. (*Hint:* trace the origins of these words.)

DISCUSSION POINT

Imagine you are asked to reform the spelling system. What changes would you make? Would you change the whole system or only part of it? What difficulties might you encounter in making your changes? If you are part of a group, you may wish to create a debate on spelling reform. Divide the group into two. One half should argue in support of spelling reform, and the other against it, defending spelling as it is now.

SUMMARY

- Spelling has become less phonemic over the years.
- A basic problem is that there are not enough letters to represent phonemes on a one-to-one basis.
- A number of oddities in spelling were introduced by ME scribes, sometimes influenced by French, and later by the early printers.
- Etymological respellings have added to the number of 'silent letters'.
- English spelling is complicated by the fact that it contains the spelling conventions of other languages.

- Beginning in the fifteenth century, a standard spelling system had fully evolved by the eighteenth century. But spellings were fixed when great changes were occurring in pronunciation, notably the Great Vowel Shift.
- Much social prestige is now attached to conforming with the standard.

FOLLOW-UP READING

The key pages on English spelling in David Crystal's *Encyclopedia of the English Language* (Cambridge: Cambridge University Press, 2003) are pp. 272–7. Also, check out the discussion of letters and sounds for OE (pp. 16–19), ME (pp. 40–3) and EMod.E (pp. 66–7 and 69); and the Great Vowel Shift is described on p. 55. The best available historical discussion of English spelling is Donald G. Scragg's *A History of English Spelling* (Manchester: Manchester University Press, 1974). For a very brief but excellent overview of English spelling (and one that demonstrates that it is less chaotic than we might think), read Edward Carney's *English Spelling is Kattastroffik* in L. Bauer and P. Trudgill's *Language Myths*, pp. 32–40 (London: Penguin, 1998). For a more comprehensive description of the sound systems of each period of English, try Jeremy Smith's *Essentials of Early English* (London: Routledge, 1999). For a snapshot of what English would have sounded like in Chaucer's day (just before the GVS), investigate the excellent Chaucer website: http://www.courses.fas.harvard.edu/~chaucer/pronunciation/. As I indicated above, Melinda Menzer's website, http://alpha.furman.edu/~mmenzer/gvs/, will make the task of understanding the GVS much easier, and, more generally for the history of the English sound system, I recommend William E. Roger's (also of Furman University) comprehensive website, http://alpha.furman.edu/~wrogers/phonemes/.

4 BORROWING WORDS

One of the most dramatic changes in the English language has been the expansion of vocabulary. In particular, this has been achieved by importing words from other languages.

The extract below is from the BBC comedy series *Yes Prime Minister*, whose principal characters are the government minister James Hacker and the civil servant Sir Humphrey. In his diary, Hacker recalls the time when Humphrey told him that he was going to move to another department:

> Humphrey had said that 'the relationship, which I might tentatively venture to aver has not been without a degree of reciprocal utility and even perhaps occasional gratification, is approaching the point of irreversible bifurcation and, to put it briefly, is in the propinquity of its ultimate regrettable termination'.
> I asked him if he would be so kind as to summarise what he's [sic] just said in words of one syllable.
> He nodded in sad acquiescence. 'I'm on my way out', he explained.
> (J. Lynn and A. Jay, *The Complete Yes Prime Minister*, London: BBC, 1989: 16)

Sir Humphrey uses a mysterious bureaucratic language to disguise the indiscretions of government and defuse any moments of potential embarrassment. Hacker is a relatively straightforward person who needs things to be put in simple language. It is almost as if they speak two different languages.

EXERCISE

4.1 Do Hacker and Humphrey speak words that come from different languages? Compare Humphrey's words quoted in the first paragraph with his words quoted in the final paragraph. Use an etymological dictionary to find out which languages these words are derived from.

There is a contrast between the loftiness of Sir Humphrey's first utterance and the mundane tone conveyed by the vocabulary of his final speech. This, as you will have discovered, can be explained by noticing that the two sets of words differ in their origin: the majority of the first set comes from Latin or French; the second set is part of the Anglo-Saxon word stock of OE, and as such it is Germanic. In the course of this unit you will find out about the different sources of our vocabulary, and about the different associations words of different origin have acquired. Keep the Indo-European family tree at the back of your mind (Appendix II).

Before beginning a brief history of English borrowing, let's note some general aspects of borrowing. The terms BORROWING and LOANWORD, referring specifically to the borrowing of a word, are misleading terms. Linguistic items are not borrowed and then given back; more accurately, they are copied by one language from another. Borrowing is not limited to one step: words are often copied by one language and then in turn copied from that language by another. Thus, the word *centre* has a borrowing path like this: ME *centre* < Old French *centre* < Latin *centrum* < Greek κεγτϱον, and so on. So, *centre* is a direct borrowing from Old French (the immediate donor language), and an indirect borrowing from the others further back in the chain. Words can be borrowed at different times with different results. One of the best examples of this is the Latin word *discus*, which has given rise to 'English' *disk, disc, dish, desk, dais* and, of course, *discus*. What kind of words are borrowed? More often nouns are borrowed than any other class of words. This is partly because nouns are the most frequent word class in any case, but also because they are relatively easy to detach from the donor language and because new things imported into a culture are often nouns. High-frequency items – articles (*the, a*), pronouns, prepositions (e.g. *of, to*), simple verbs, kinship terms, body parts – are less likely to be borrowed. Is it only words that are borrowed? Borrowing occurs at all levels (all examples are French (Fr.) borrowings):

Borrowing
Loanword

Graphic elements:	e.g. diacritics – *gâteau, café*
Phonic elements:	e.g. the diphthong [ɔɪ] (as in *joy, cloister*)
Morphemes:	e.g. *gâteau* – *gâteaux* (the plural marker <x> is borrowed); *kitchen* + *ette* > *kitchenette* (the suffix *-ette* is borrowed)
Words:	see examples in the commentary below
Phrases:	e.g. *au fait, raison d'être, joie de vivre*
Sentences:	e.g. *Je ne sais quoi*

Why does borrowing take place? The reasons, all of which were touched on in Unit 2, will become clear in our brief survey of English borrowing below. In short, borrowing is facilitated by languages coming into contact; changes in the environment, including cultural changes, creating a need for new vocabulary; and speakers wanting to use the vocabulary of a prestigious language to improve, for example, their social status.

Even before the supposed Angles, Saxons and Jutes arrived in England bringing their Germanic dialects that gave rise to English, they had borrowed some Latin vocabulary. However, as far as we know, this amounted to only a few dozen words (e.g. *wall, street, cheap, wine*), and thus OE vocabulary was overwhelmingly Germanic. OE contained very few loanwords, contrasting with the situation in ME and Mod.E, where loans proliferate. One estimate is that 3 per cent of OE vocabulary consisted of loanwords, whereas 70 per cent of today's English consists of loanwords. This difference is of great importance in explaining how the English language has changed over time.

Many Germanic Anglo-Saxon words have survived into Mod.E with very little change in either form or meaning (e.g. *god, gold, hand, land, under, winter, word*). The majority of the few loanwords in OE were from Latin. This is no great surprise, given the fact that religious texts were written in Latin and the early Christian missionaries were influential in spreading literacy. They introduced some 450 Latin words into the language, mainly to do with the Church (e.g. *altar, angel, cleric, nun, temple, psalm, master, demon*).

The Scandinavian Vikings invaded and settled in England from the ninth to the eleventh centuries. Anglo-Saxon English and the Scandinavian languages (Old Norse and Old Danish) were all Germanic languages, and to some extent mutually comprehensible. This close similarity made it easier to adopt words into all areas of vocabulary (e.g. *are, die, leg, want, get, both, give, same, they, them, their*), not just words with specialised content, such as religious vocabulary. One estimate is that 1,800 words of Scandinavian origin have survived into present-day English, including very common words. The word *are*, for example, became part of the verb *to be* – the most common verb in English. (Note the use of *are* in the word-for-word translation of Text 1 (Appendix IV), where it replaces the Anglo-Saxon word *sind*.)

After the Norman invasion of 1066, French became the official language of law and administration. The ruling groups spoke French, and popularised French dress, cooking and etiquette. Even when English displaced French after about 200 years, prestigious French culture exerted a powerful influence. Some estimate that over 10,000 words were adopted from French during the ME period (e.g. *parliament, baron, manor, noble, liberty, government, arrest, judge, jury, prison, beef, lettuce, mutton, pork, sausage, dress, jewel, cloak, virtue, art, beauty, romance*). In many cases OE words were replaced by French ones (e.g. OE *stow* – Fr. *place*, OE *wyrd* – Fr. *fortune*). Interestingly, where both survived, sometimes meanings would drift apart. Consider the pairs OE *house* – Fr. *mansion* and OE *bloody* – Fr. *sanguine*. The SEMANTIC or meaning system did not need two words doing the same job, and so one changed.

Semantic

An enormous number of the French borrowings had originally come from Latin. There were also several thousand direct Latin borrowings into English, particularly towards the end of the ME period. Most of these were from areas such as religion, science, law and literature (e.g. *scripture, client, conviction, library, scribe, dissolve, quadrant, medicine, ulcer*). However, it was not until the Renaissance in the sixteenth century that borrowing from Latin took off. The Renaissance saw the development of new concepts and techniques and the flowering of the arts and sciences, as well as further exploration of the world (Renaissance means 'rebirth', referring to this cultural rebirth). Much of this took place on the continent of Europe. Learning was given a boost by printing, and books became widely available. However, many literary, scientific and religious texts were in Latin, since Latin was the language of scholarship and scholarly literature. To make these texts more widely available, people began to translate them into English, often using a Latin word in the translation when no good English equivalent could be found. The upshot of these developments was that words from many languages were adopted into English, but especially words from Latin and the Romance languages French, Italian and Spanish. One estimate is that 13,000 new loanwords entered the language in the sixteenth century alone, and of these some 7,000 were from Latin. Examples of Latin loanwords include *absurdity, benefit, exist, exaggerate, external, obstruction, relaxation, relevant, vacuum, virus, excursion, fact, impersonal, expectation, exact* and *eradicate*.

More recently, there seems to be a general decline in borrowing from Classical and Romance languages. French borrowing has been in decline since the ME period, and Latin since the end of the seventeenth century. Why is this? One possible reason is that these languages experienced a decline in prestige: towards the end of the ME period, the upper classes ceased to speak French, and English became the language of administration; towards the end of the seventeenth century, English took over from Latin as the language of scholarship. We might note here that English is now itself generally the most prestigious language in the world. Another reason is that English has gone global: it comes into contact with languages right round the world. As a consequence, English is now borrowing from languages that have not been traditional sources for vocabulary. For example, one study suggests that Japanese accounted for 8 per cent of borrowings in the last 50 years, and African languages for 6 per cent. A further reason is that, although borrowing from other languages used to be an important source for new words, it is now of relatively minor importance, accounting for around 4 per cent of new words. Nowadays most new words are formed from the resources we already have, by compounding words, for example. We will consider such word creation in the next unit.

Today, it is clear that Germanic, French or Latin vocabulary has acquired a distinctive flavour of its own, and is used in different contexts and for different purposes.

EXERCISE

4.2 (a) What impression do the extracts in Texts 8(a) and (b) (Appendix IV) give? Describe the vocabulary used (use an etymological dictionary to trace the origins of the words). Why is this particular vocabulary used in these particular extracts?

(b) Using an etymological dictionary, compare the vocabulary of Text 4 with the vocabulary of Text 7. Why is this particular vocabulary used in these particular extracts?

Consider these stylistic scales:

Germanic		*Latin*
Spoken	↔	Written
Frequent	↔	Rare
Informal	↔	Formal
Private	↔	Public
Simple (monosyllabic)	↔	Complex (polysyllabic)
Affective	↔	Neutral
Concrete	↔	Abstract

To clarify, Germanic words often express some kind of attitude, whether negative or positive, whereas Latin words tend to be more neutral (compare the pair: *cheap – inexpensive*). They also often refer to concrete things (e.g. *wood, earth, house, pot, pan, knife, fork*), while Latin words tend to refer to more abstract concepts. In sum, Germanic vocabulary is the stuff of everyday conversations, containing frequent, informal, private, simple and affective items, while Latinate vocabulary tends towards the opposite, the language of formal writing. In terms of these scales, French words tend to lie between Germanic and Latinate vocabulary.

An important issue is *why* these areas of vocabulary have acquired particular characteristics. This can be explained by looking at the historical development of English loanwords. The bulk of Latin vocabulary entered the language during the Renaissance, a period of lexical upheaval. The important point is that, unlike the earlier borrowing of French vocabulary into speech, Latin vocabulary was the language of the written medium, the language of books or the 'inkhorn' (= a horn containing ink, i.e. an inkwell). Much of it was difficult to understand (and still is!), and was perceived as 'alien' by some. Not surprisingly, it is in the early seventeenth century that the first dictionaries appeared, in order to help people cope with these 'hard words'. This state of affairs gave rise to the so-called INKHORN CONTROVERSY, a debate about the merits or otherwise of the acquisition of 'artificial', 'bookish' Latin vocabulary – the vocabulary coming from the inkhorn – in place of 'natural', 'common' Germanic vocabulary.

Inkhorn Controversy

Some strands of the Inkhorn Controversy are still current today. The quest for a pure Anglo-Saxon vocabulary has continued over the centuries. However, as we have seen, there never was a pure Anglo-Saxon vocabulary: Latin loanwords were part of English vocabulary even before English came to England. A more practical consideration – and one that will become clear in the following unit – is that Latin and Germanic vocabulary are so thoroughly mixed that they would be very difficult to separate.

EXERCISES

4.3 Read through the list of words below and give a rating out of five for each word, according to how formal you think it is (0 = very informal, 5 = very formal). (*Hint:* Think about whether you have come across the word before, and, if so, how formal the context was (e.g. ordinary conversation, religious or legal texts).)

fire	=	fear	=
holy	=	ascend	=
trepidation	=	flame	=
rise	=	sacred	=
conflagration	=	terror	=
mount	=	consecrated	=

Now rearrange the words above to form four rows of synonyms (i.e. words of similar meaning). Organise your rows so that they are in columns according to language of origin (e.g. Germanic, French or Latin). (Use an etymological dictionary to find this information.)

	Germanic	*French*	*Latin*
1			
2			
3			
4			

How does etymology correlate with formality? If you can, check your ratings with someone else's.

4.4 Keith Waterhouse, a contemporary commentator on the English language, offers advice about which words to use in his book *English our English* (Harmondsworth: Penguin, 1991). This advice, part of which is given in the bullet points below, echoes the dictates of previous commentators such as George Orwell and Henry W. Fowler. What seems to be the underlying basis for his advice? (*Hint:* consider the origins of the words he focuses on.) Are these words synonymous, as he implies – can we simply use one for the other? Is his advice helpful?

- Prefer short, plain words to long, college-educated ones. *End*, not *terminate*.
- Use concrete words, not abstract ones. *Rain*, not *inclement weather*.
- Avoid abstract adjectives. *Penniless*, not *penurious*.
- Do not use foreign words if you can help it. *£20,000 a year*, not *£20,000 per annum*.

DISCUSSION POINT

Sometimes present-day debates about keeping English plain and simple sound rather similar to the Inkhorn Controversy. What are the positive or negative aspects of using Latin or Germanic vocabulary? Can the avoidance of Latin vocabulary be helpful? Or, does the avoidance of Latin vocabulary have some negative consequences? In what way does it depend on what you are trying to do with your language (give some examples)? If you are part of a group, set up a debate: half argue for Germanic vocabulary and half for Latin vocabulary.

SUMMARY

- The dramatic expansion of English vocabulary has been achieved through loanwords, mostly from French and Latin but also from Greek, Italian and Spanish.
- It has been facilitated by contact between languages, the attraction of prestigious languages and environmental, including cultural, changes.
- In more recent times, English has borrowed from a more diverse range of languages, and, more generally, borrowing as a method of increasing vocabulary has become less important.
- English words of different origin have acquired different stylistic associations, and tend to be used in different contexts.
- People have particular attitudes to words of different origin.

FOLLOW-UP READING

The key pages in David Crystal's *Encyclopedia of the English Language* (Cambridge: Cambridge University Press, 2003) are pp. 8, 24–7, 60–1 and 124–7. Most of the standard history of the English language textbooks contain a relevant section. Extensive standard works on the subject include J.A. Sheard's *The Words of English* (New York: W.W. Norton, 1966) and Mary S. Serjeantson's *A History of Foreign Words in English* (London: Routledge & Kegan Paul, [1935] 1961). However, the most comprehensive up-to-date discussion of English vocabulary (and a mine of interest) is Geoffrey's Hughes's *A History of English Words* (Oxford: Blackwell, 2000). If you are curious about the cosmopolitan make-up of the English lexicon, explore http://www.wordorigins.org/loanword.htm.

5 NEW WORDS FROM OLD

One way of creating new vocabulary has been to use already existing words or word-elements. Over time, this method has become increasingly important.

Where do new words come from? In the last unit we looked at words borrowed from other languages, and in this unit we are going to look at how new words have been created from old. However, you may be wondering about words that are completely original creations, words that have no roots. The fact of the matter is that these are few and far between. One estimate is that below half a per cent of new vocabulary over the last 50 years is original. *Googol* – the word for the number 1 followed by a hundred zeros – is an example. It was brought into the world by a nine-year-old boy, Milton Sirotta, when his father, the mathematician Edward Kasner, asked him for a suitable name for that number (it later inspired the name of the internet search engine google.com). Some rootless words are supposed to have been created to represent sounds – they are echoic or ONOMATOPOEIC. *Cuckoo* is the classic example and there are many others (e.g. *bleep, honk, bang*). Rootless words tend to crop up in literary texts, particularly fantasy and science fiction, but they rarely move into common usage, exceptions perhaps being *hobbit* and *triffid*. The point is that the vast majority of words have some kind of etymology – they have roots.

Onomatopoeic

How are words formed from the resources that we already have? Below is a checklist that outlines some of the ways in which words are formed. *Affixation – adding affixes to form another word.* Affixes are short elements that usually do not exist as words in their own right, but are tacked on to a root word in order to form another. Affixes that are placed at the beginning of a word are called PREFIXES (e.g. *undress, decompose, misfortune, recall*) and affixes placed at the end of a word are called

Prefixes

SUFFIXES (e.g. *troublesome, harmonise, singer, sinful*). OE was well **Suffixes** stocked with affixes, some of which are still among the most commonly used in English (e.g. *happy, quickly, blackness, foolish, heartless*). Affixes vary in terms of how PRODUCTIVE they are. Some OE affixes are no **Productive** longer used or are falling out of use. For instance, the prefix *for-* and the suffix *-lock* were once relatively frequently used, but now are largely confined to the words *forgive, forgo, forbid, forbear, forlorn, forsake* and *forswear*, and *wedlock* and *warlock*. Other OE affixes fell out of use, but then experienced a revival. This happened to both *-dom* and *-wise*, which reappeared in words like *stardom, officialdom* and *likewise* – a revival that in both cases was led by American English. The major change in English affixes over time has been expansion due to the acquisition of affixes from other languages. Just as English borrowed words, it also borrowed affixes. Examples include *anti-, -ism* and *micro-* from Greek (e.g. **anti**climax, Communism, **micro**wave), *-al, ex-, multi-, non-* and *re-* from Latin (e.g. *accidental, exchange, **multi**racial, **non**-stop* and **re**build), and *-ette* and *-esque* from French (e.g. *kitchenette* and *picturesque*).

EXERCISE

5.1 More than one affix can be used to create a word. How many affixes are in the following word, and from which languages have they been borrowed?

   antidisestablishmentarianism

   (*Hint:* Remember that many etymological dictionaries list affixes as well as words, so you can check that what you think is an affix really is an affix, and also find out what it means and/or what it does.) Affixes can bring about a change in meaning or a change in grammar (e.g. the addition of *-ness* to the word *happy* results in a change from adjective to noun). Beginning with the root word *establish*, add on affixes and each time describe what changes occur.

BACK FORMATION – *subtracting elements (often affixes) to form another* **Back formation** *word*. For example, the word *editor* appeared before the word *edit*. With the subtraction of the affix *-or*, English gained the word *edit*, the verb describing what the editor does. Similarly, *burglar* came before the verb *burgle*. An interesting example of back formation is the word *pea*, which comes from *pease*. Originally, *pease* was both the singular and

the plural. However, because it sounded as if it had a plural ending, people invented *pea* to talk about a single pea.

Compounding

COMPOUNDING – *combining words to form another word.* We met the process of compounding in Unit 1. There are, in fact, three forms of compound: there are open compounds (e.g. *new born*), hyphenated compounds (e.g. *new-born*) and solid compounds (e.g. *newborn*). These compounding conventions are somewhat arbitrary, and there are differences between British and American English (for example, American English seems to avoid hyphenated forms). But, generally, older and shorter compounds are more likely to be solid. The above example is more likely to be solid than the more recent compounds *new town* or *new wave*. In fact, some very old compounds are barely recognisable as such. The word *lord* is an example. It began life as the compound *hlaf-weard*, meaning 'loaf-keeper', but even in OE it had contracted to *hlaford*.

EXERCISES

5.2 Use an etymological dictionary to discover the words involved in the following compounds:

lady, gossip, daisy, nostril, sheriff, goodbye

5.3 How old is the open compound *acid rain?* Have a guess. Now go and use an etymological dictionary to see whether you were right. It is very difficult to guess accurately the age of new words. Sometimes apparently new words have been lurking for years at the edges of vocabulary – often as specialised vocabulary – and only later make their way into mainstream usage. Computer terminology, for example, seems fairly new. However, most of it was coined in the 1950s and 1960s, and only with the advent of the PC in the 1980s did it become mainstream vocabulary.

5.4 Investigate Texts 3 and 4 (Appendix IV) for examples of words that are today solid compounds but are here represented as open.

Blends

BLENDS – *fusing elements of two other words.* In a sense, this is an extreme form of compounding. Classic examples include *smoke + fog > smog, motor*

+ *hotel* > *motel*; *breakfast* + *lunch* > *brunch*. Importantly, such blending of words occurs at the time the word is formed, and thus it is distinguished from a word like *lord* where fusion occurs over time.

FUNCTIONAL CONVERSION – using one part of speech as another. For example, consider the conversion of nouns into verbs, or, more specifically, body-part nouns that have been used as verbs: to *head* a department, to *eye* someone up, to *nose* into somebody's affairs, to *neck* with someone, to *shoulder* or *elbow* somebody aside, to *hand* in an assignment, to *finger* one's watch, to *leg* it, to *knee* someone in the . . ., and so on. Shakespeare added 'to *lip* a wanton wench', though this did not gain general currency. Not only can nouns be converted into verbs, but it seems that almost any part of speech can be used as another. The words *up* and *down* would seem to be fairly limited words, but they too can be converted into nouns, as in expressions like *I'm coping with the ups and downs of life.*

Functional conversion

EXERCISE

5.5 One kind of functional conversion is when personal names (proper nouns) are converted into other types of word. A surprising number of such words or EPONYMS have been created this way. Use an etymological dictionary to find out which people gave their names to the following words: *lynch, dunce, boycott, sandwich, cardigan, wellingtons, pasteurise, sadism, atlas, jovial, venereal, tantalise.*

Eponyms

CLIPS – shortening a longer word (usually by removing syllables). Clips involve the creation of a new shortened form of a word, which, in most cases, supplants the original word. Thus, we talk about a *bus* rather than an *omnibus*. For some peculiar reason, the set of vocabulary related to underwear consists largely of clips: *vestment* > *vest, pantaloons* > *pants, knickerbockers* > *knickers, brassière* > *bra.* Interestingly, British and American English sometimes varies with regard to the extent of a clip. Compare *advert* and *ad.*

Clips

ACRONYMS – combining the initial letters of words or syllables. Some words are quite clearly acronyms, for example *TV* (*television*), *TB* (*tuberculosis*), *VD* (*venereal disease*), and *DIY* (*do it yourself*). Other words are less transparently acronyms, for example *radar* (*radio detecting and ranging*) and *laser* (*light amplification by stimulated emission of radiation*).

Acronyms

There are two important points to bear in mind about these ways in which words can be created. First, they can overlap, or a word can switch from one to another. There are a number of affixes, for example, which can also function as independent words, and so sometimes it is not clear whether, say, affixation or compounding is involved. There is an issue, for example, with the suffix *-able*. The suffix is actually a borrowing of the Latin suffix *-ibilis*, which in French and later in English was sometimes spelt *-able*. However, in form it is identical to the adjective *able* (e.g. *He is able to do it*), which comes via French from the Latin word *habilem*. Thus, with relatively recent words ending *-able* (e.g. *analysable*, *killable*), it is not clear whether we should analyse them as affixation or compounding. Sometimes, during the history of a particular word, an element can change status (at least in the mind of the analyser). Think about the word *outrage*. How would you analyse it? It's a compound, *out + rage* – right? This is always the unanimous verdict of my students. And they wouldn't be wrong now. But *outrage* started life as an Old French loanword. Originally, the boundary was *outr + -age*, which in turn had been formed from Latin *ultra + -aticum*. Note here that *-age* is a productive affix, which is also used in words like *savage*, *language*, *baggage* and, more recently, *outage*. And so *outrage* came about through affixation. Not surprisingly, given that the sense of Latin *ultra* is 'beyond', it meant 'going beyond the bounds, being excessive'. However,

Reanalysis *outrage* underwent what is termed REANALYSIS. People came to perceive it as having a different structure: *out + rage* – a compound. This word reanalysis went hand-in-hand with the development in meaning. *Outrage* used to mean going beyond the bounds, whatever those bounds might be (e.g. excessive boldness, luxury); now, it refers more specifically to a violent act that goes beyond the bounds of ordered, normal behaviour (e.g. a terrorist bomb attack). Clearly, the sense of violent behaviour is one that has been promoted by the perception of 'rage' as the second word in the compound.

Second, these ways of creating words are not equally productive in generating vocabulary. Consider these approximate figures (conflated from various studies) for sources of new vocabulary over the last 50 years:

Compounding	36%
Affixation	27%
Functional conversion	17%
Shortening (back formations, clips, acronyms)	9%
Blending	6%

In fact, compounding used to be even more important in English. As an illustration of this, consider the selection of OE compounds below, all formed with *folc* ('folk') meaning 'people' or 'tribe', and note how the present-day equivalents are words that have been borrowed from French or Latin.

OE compound	Literal translation	Present-day equivalent
folclar	people preaching	homily (Fr.)
folcmære	people famous	celebrated (L.)
folcscipe	people ship	nation (Fr.)
folcslite	people bite	sedition (Fr.)
folctalu	people tale	genealogy (Fr.)
folcweleg	people rich	populous (L.)

This is not surprising, given that compounding is popular in Germanic languages and that English used to be more Germanic in character. With the great influx of loanwords, the development of English, unlike that of Modern German, did not have to rely so much on internal resources. For example, English adopted the word *bra* (*brassière*) from French; Modern German has the compound *büstenhalter* (literally, 'bust-holder').

What types of language contain many new word formations? Literary texts are often said to be a source. In particular, Shakespeare is credited with many coinages, though one can never be entirely sure whether he really invented them or whether he was simply the first person to record what was already in the language (particularly spoken language). For example, by adding the affix *-less*, he made an adjective out of the verb *to count* in the line 'One sweet kiss shall pay this *countless* debt.' A new coinage, such as this, which enters the general word stock, is called a NEOLOGISM. However, many words are formed for the 'nonce': they are one-off coinages for the particular purpose in hand; they tend to have relatively limited circulation and are quickly forgotten. These are called NONCE-FORMATIONS. For instance, Shakespeare's line 'Would'st thou be window'd [i.e. placed in a window] in great Rome' contains the nonce-formation *window'd*; though we now can talk about *framing* somebody, we cannot talk about 'windowing' them. As with literary texts, the language of advertising often displays word-formation creativity in an attempt to capture the reader's attention. Sometimes product names enter the language as general vocabulary items. Consider terms for adhesive tape: *Scotch tape* (common in the United States) and *Sellotape* (common in the United Kingdom) are both registered trademarks.

Neologism

Nonce-formations

Throughout the centuries people have expressed negative attitudes to certain word-forms. Today, one still finds people writing to newspapers or television stations with their objections. In particular, hybrid forms, such as *television* (Greek *tele* + Latin *vision*) or *officialdom* (Latin *official* + OE *dom*), have been criticised. Sometimes prejudices are expressed against particular affixes. The verb-forming suffix *-ise* (or *-ize*) in words like *finalise*, *prioritise* and *routinise* often provokes anger. From a linguistic point of view, there is nothing that makes these word-forms better or worse than others. The issue is a social one. As I hinted in Unit 2, people tend to be conservative and dislike change of any kind. Over time people accept innovations. For example, the word *beefeater*, which is now very much part of the establishment, is in fact a hybrid form: French *beef* + Germanic *eater*.

EXERCISES

5.6   I have selected ten words for each of the twentieth, seven-teenth, fourteenth and eleventh centuries from the *OED*, paying little attention to how the words came to exist in English. Go through the lists below and label the words using the same categories as above (i.e. affixation, back formation, compounding, blending, functional conversion, clipping, and, from Unit 4, borrowing). You will also need an additional category 'OE', for words that have neither been borrowed into English nor created within it, but are part of the orig-inal Anglo-Saxon word-stock. For instances of borrowing, also note which was the direct donor language, but don't try and trace the etymology of the words right back. For example, *introspect* is a seventeenth-century borrowing from Latin, and, for the purposes of this exercise, you can label it as such. However, if one went further back, one would find that it originated in Latin through a process of affixation: *intro-* (meaning 'inside') plus *spicere* (meaning 'to look').

Twentieth century	Seventeenth century	Fourteenth century	Eleventh century
AIDS	antihypnotic	ability	afterward
backslash	brilliant	colony	climb
Rambo	homework	colourless	consul
camcorder	introspect	communication	coolness
upgradable	delinquence	handmaid	guilty
buyout	diagnosis	labour	marshmallow
mousse (verb)	enema	predicament	millstone
trueish	piano	pupil	shepherd
perestroika	undercurrent	presently	shorten
spreadsheet	manufacture (verb)	sixpence	undergo

Look across the centuries to see how frequently words were created via a particular process. Bear in mind that the sample of words you have for each century is extremely small, so concentrate on the bigger differences. What changes have occurred? In the light of the commentary in this and the last unit, can you explain why these changes have occurred?

5.7 How are the most recent additions to English coming about? I think some of the most recent additions include: *snail mail*, *road rage*, *way* (as in 'way cool'), *detox*, *fantabulous* and *IMHO*. Account for these. You can always investigate other examples of new words. Several websites list what they think are new words (search on 'new words'). You could also investigate the 'Word of the Day' at http://www.oed.com/ (and have new words/senses e-mailed to you for free).

DISCUSSION POINT

Think of as many new word-forms as you can. Now go and check them in a dictionary. Are they genuinely new or are they just, for example, colloquial forms that have been in the language for years? If you are part of a group, set up a competition to think up the newest word-forms.

SUMMARY

- Few English words are original creations; most are borrowed from other languages or formed from existing vocabulary.
- The most important processes of word formation in English are compounding, affixation and functional conversion.
- Compounding was the most important way of generating new vocabulary in OE. In the history of English, compounding seems to decrease in importance when borrowing increases.
- English has significantly increased its stock of affixes by borrowing from other languages.
- Words are formed with no apparent regard as to where the original elements come from, resulting in hybrid forms. These, as well as other new forms, have been the subject of complaint.

FOLLOW-UP READING

The key pages in David Crystal's *Encyclopedia of the English Language* (Cambridge: Cambridge University Press, 2003) are pp. 128–35. Also, check out the relevant sections on pp. 22, 61 and 198. Thomas Pyles and John Algeo give a good overview in *The Origins and Development of the English Language* (Fort Worth, TX: Harcourt Brace Jovanovich, 2004). Parts of Francis Katamba's *English Words* (London: Routledge, 2004), though rather more advanced, are also worth trying. If you are interested in words created from names, have a look at C.L. Beeching's *Dictionary of Eponyms* (London: Library Association, 1989); if you are interested in new words, try browsing through the *Oxford Dictionary of New Words* (1998), or one of the many websites listing new words. *World Wide Words* at http://www.quinion.com/words/index.php is a particularly good general source of information about words.

CHANGING MEANINGS

6

Changes in the meanings of words – semantic change – can be among the most striking and accessible examples of language change. However, one needs to be aware that meanings are subtle and complex, and not simply captured within a dictionary-type definition.

If you want to find out what a word means, what do you do? Most people would look the word up in a dictionary. Dictionaries can indeed shed light on meanings and how they arose, but must be treated with caution, because word meaning is more than a compact definition of the type we see in dictionaries. Word meaning, one might say, is like an onion. First, it consists of many layers. Words typically have POLYSEMY – a range of different meanings. For example, the word *set* has at least 36 senses (try looking it up in a dictionary; you'll find that different dictionaries represent different numbers of senses). Second, just as an onion's taste will vary according to how people use it – whether in a curry sauce or a bolognaise sauce – the meanings of words vary according to use. Knowing the meaning of a word is knowing how it is used. As words become used in different ways and in different contexts, they acquire different associations and so the meaning changes.

Polysemy

EXERCISE

6.1 If we had to think of a list of features or criteria that defined both the words *woman* and *lady*, one might suggest that they include being human, female and adult. A definition based on these lines would be the DENOTATIVE MEANING of the two

Denotative meaning

words. But there must be more to meaning than this, since we know that there is a difference between these two words – we know they can be used to mean different things. Consider these words placed in the context of the sentences below.

She's only thirteen, but she's a woman already
She's only thirteen, but she's a lady already

Connotations

What differences in meaning – what different associations or CONNOTATIONS – do the words have?

One way in which dictionaries try to give us clues about usage is by providing quotations where the word is used. However, even the dictionaries that do contain quotations cannot, for practical reasons, contain every usage of a word. It becomes a matter of selection and interpretation by the editor, and inevitably dictionaries lag behind actual usage. Also, dictionaries, particularly traditional ones, tend to underplay associative meaning. In fact, often the associative meaning of a word becomes the central meaning of a word. For example, *sinister*, a borrowing from Latin, originally meant 'left' or 'left hand'. But even in Latin it had associations of bad luck. By the seventeenth century these associations formed the denotative meaning of the word, the notion of 'leftness' having died out.

Etymological meaning

One particular area of meaning we need to note is ETYMOLOGICAL MEANING. This is precisely the kind of meaning we examined in Unit 1, where we tried to uncover the earlier meanings of particular words. The important point here is that people generally assume that the earlier meaning of a word is the 'correct' and legitimate one. Consider this statement:

Decimate means to destroy a proportion (originally a tenth) of a group of people or things, not to destroy them all or nearly all.
(*The Economist Style Sheet*, 1986)

It articulates a prescriptive view, but not a view that reflects how language really works. I defy anybody to go out and use *decimate* with the etymological meaning dictated. People would not understand you, because word meanings are shared conventions not gold standards to be imposed. But the myth of the etymological meaning being the 'right one' endures in the prescriptive tradition.

What words can change meaning and why do they change? All words can change meaning. Even words that seem to be more grammatical in character can change. The word *and* used to mean 'in the presence of', as in this text: 'Hæfdon gleám and dreám *and* heora ordfruman' (Cædmon, *c.* 1000) ('They have joy and mirth *in the presence of* their creator'). Now, *and* is a conjunction – it glues sentences or bits of sentences together (look at the first sentence of this paragraph). However, some words are rather more stable than others. For example, words for basic elements (e.g. kinship terms – *mother, father,* and so on) tend to be relatively stable, whereas words expressing evaluations (e.g. intensifiers – 'it's *dead/way/real* cool') have usually experienced rapid change at some point. As for why words change meaning, we can refer to the general reasons given in Unit 2, but it will help to develop this further. Meanings change – as indeed does language generally – as part (even if only a subconscious part) of communication. Let's break communication down into various components and relate this to changes in word meaning:

Communicative component	Motivation	Example
Context	New need	A pervasive factor. For example, *video* (as a noun) was first used with the advent of television in the 1930s to refer to what was displayed on a television screen; it then was used for a video recorder, which was developed in the 1950s; and today it is most frequently used for the videotape cassette, which was popularised in the 1980s.
Language	Competing words	See the discussion of *house – mansion* and *bloody – sanguine* in Unit 4, where new French loanwords seem to have caused a shift in the meaning of OE words.
Speaker	Innovative use	An important factor, especially observable in genres such as slang. Consider the use of *bad* or *wicked* to mean *good*.
Hearer	Innovative interpretation	This can include 'misinterpretations' and 'reinterpretations'. See the example of *outrage* in Unit 5.

New meanings do not come out of nowhere but are most often developments or extensions of earlier meanings. A traditional way of categorising the ways in which words may change meaning is the following:

SPECIALISATION – *narrowing of meaning.* For example, the word *meat* used to refer to any kind of food, but now refers specifically to flesh. (Check the meaning of *mete* 'meat' in Text 3 (Appendix IV).) The word *deer* used to refer to any kind of beast, but now refers to a particular four-legged wild animal.

Specialisation

Generalisation GENERALISATION – *widening of meaning*. For example, the word *business* originally meant 'a state of being active', but the meaning was extended over time to include 'occupation', 'a piece of work', 'a concern, matter, affair', 'dealings', 'trade' and 'a commercial enterprise'.

Amelioration AMELIORATION – *elevation of meaning*. For example, the word *pretty* began with the negative sense of 'cunning, crafty', and the word *shrewd* began with the negative sense of 'depraved, wicked'.

Pejoration PEJORATION – *degradation of meaning*. King James II (1685–8), upon seeing the new St Paul's cathedral, described it as 'amusing, awful and artificial', by which he meant it was wonderful. *Amusing* had the sense of capturing one's attention; *awful* of being impressive, majestic (literally, full of awe); and *artificial* of being skilful, displaying art.

Transfer TRANSFER *of meaning*. Sometimes the meaning of a word shifts, so that the word refers to a different – though often closely associated – set of things. For example, the list below charts the main shifts in the meaning of the word *bureau* (drawn from Nerlich, B. and Nerlich, D.D., 'Semantic change: case studies based on traditional and cognitive semantics', *Journal of Literary Semantics*, 1992, 21, 204–25: 208):

twelfth century	coarse woollen cloth
thirteenth century	cloth covering tables or counters
fourteenth century	counting table
fifteenth/sixteenth century	writing table
seventeenth century	room containing the table
	people working in the room
	department
	agency

Another particularly pervasive way in which meaning can change – and one which underlies some of the examples discussed above – is through **Metaphor** METAPHOR. A metaphor involves talking about something in terms of something else.

EXERCISE

6.2 Spot the metaphor: look through the list below and tick the examples which you think contain a metaphor.

(a) My teacher is a wonderful person.

(b) My teacher is an encyclopedia.

(c) My teacher causes daily earthquakes in the classroom.
(d) My teacher frightens me enormously.
(e) My teacher never runs out of batteries (I wish I could find the off button).
(f) My teacher is definitely not good-looking.
(g) My teacher talks in fast forward.
(h) My teacher fills my days with light.

Sometimes the meaning of a word involves a CONVENTIONAL METAPHOR: the metaphorical meaning is conventionalised or lexicalised, so that it might be included in a dictionary. For example, if I ask you the question 'Have you *grasped* what I'm writing about?', I am not talking about you physically 'grabbing' hold of something but about you 'understanding' something. The metaphorical meaning of 'understanding' is derived from the physical meaning of 'grabbing', but in interpreting my question it is highly likely that you went immediately for the conventional meaning 'understand', without any consideration of the physical meaning. Other times the literal meaning of a word falls into disuse and only the metaphorical meaning survives. In this case we have a DEAD METAPHOR. For instance, the word *candid* now means 'frank, open, not hiding one's thoughts', but in its earliest history in English it could mean 'white' – the sense of the Latin word *candidus* from which it is derived. In contrast, the physical meaning of grasp is still current (e.g. 'I grasped his hand'), so the metaphor is not dead.

Conventional metaphor

Dead metaphor

EXERCISE

6.3 Using an etymological dictionary, investigate the dead metaphors in *comprehend, dilapidated, dependent, petrified*.

Of course, the above ways in which words have changed meaning, though fairly comprehensive, is not complete. Also, remember that some words can be classified along a number of different dimensions, and sometimes words shift their meaning as part of a set of words. In fact, some of the most interesting changes in word meaning have taken place in whole sets of related words.

EXERCISE

6.4 The development of terms used to refer to women is particularly interesting. Using a dictionary with etymological information or a specialist etymological dictionary, investigate the meaning of the words below. In particular, consider whether it has always been the case that these words only refer to women, and whether they originally had a neutral or favourable meaning, but have experienced pejoration.

dragon, hag, harpy, hussy, minx, mistress, scold, shrew, witch

Looking at changes in whole sets of words can lead to some interesting observations about semantic change in general, observations that suggest semantic change is not random but regular and systematic. A leading authority in this area is Elizabeth C. Traugott. She suggested specific directions in which words tend to change meaning. I do not have space to outline this in detail, but the summary below gives the flavour of her findings. Meanings tend to change in the following directions (the tendencies can overlap and I have simplified their labels):

Towards more abstract meanings. For example, the word *bureau* (discussed above) changed from something quite physical, something touchable (a cloth), to something that is abstract and untouchable (an agency).

Towards more textual meanings. For example, the word *and* (discussed above) originally meant 'in the presence of' – it told us about the position of something, just as do the words *by, next, in front of,* etc. (these are all spatial prepositions). But it is now used to join two bits of text (it is now primarily a conjunction).

Towards more self-oriented meanings. For example, the word *well* has changed from meaning a positive state (e.g. good fortune, health), which it can still do today, to also being able to mark the speaker's attitudes and beliefs about something, as when one says 'Well I never!'.

DISCUSSION POINT

Are there word meanings you have used – or you have seen or heard used – that have been criticised (perhaps by a parent or a teacher)? For example, some people object to the use of the word *aggravation* to mean 'trouble caused by aggressive behaviour or harassment'. Talk to some other people, in order to compile a list of 'pet hates'. Why do you think people object to these meanings? How do they justify their objections? Do they appeal to a particular authority? Do you agree with them?

SUMMARY

* Dictionaries are an important resource in discovering the meanings of words, but a dictionary is not the ultimate authority: it is shaped by the attitudes, abilities and policies of the editor and the compilers.
* The meaning of a word is not simply a list of distinctive features, the denotative meaning, but includes the equally important associative meaning, acquired according to how a word is used.
* All kinds of words change meaning, though some are more stable than others.
* Words change meaning as a consequence of their use in communication.
* Some of the traditional ways in which shifts in meaning have been classified include specialisation, generalisation, amelioration, pejoration and transfer. Metaphor is a particularly pervasive mechanism underlying meaning change.
* More systematic directions for meaning change have been suggested, such as the tendency to move towards more abstract, textual and/or self-oriented meanings.

FOLLOW-UP READING

The key pages in David Crystal's *Encyclopedia of the English Language* (Cambridge: Cambridge University Press, 2003) are pp. 138–9, and pp. 170–3 are also relevant. Most textbooks on the history of the English language contain a section on meaning or semantic change. There are also more specialised books that deal with meaning changes within particular words (e.g. Adrian Room's *N.T.C.'s Dictionary of Changes in Meaning* (London: Routledge, 1996), or James Copley's *Shift of Meaning* (Oxford: Oxford University Press, 1961)). If you're interested in the history of words referring to women, try Chapter 10 of Geoffrey Hughes's *Swearing: A Social History of Foul Language, Oaths and Profanity in English* (Oxford: Blackwell, 1991). All of Elizabeth C. Traugott's writings on semantic change are advanced, but they are clear and so you should be able to get the gist. Try: 'From propositional to textual and expressive meanings; some semantic-pragmatic aspects of grammaticalization', in Wilfred P. Lehmann and Yakov Malkiel (eds) *Perspective on Historical Linguistics*, (Amsterdam: Benjamins, 1982), pp. 245–71.

7 GRAMMAR I

Nouns

> Over many centuries, English has undergone an important shift in the way it signals grammatical information. The legacy of the past is still apparent in irregular plurals (e.g. mice, sheep) and the apostrophe-s (e.g. Jonathan's book).

Since the eighteenth century, grammar has been mystified or made into a kind of mental assault course, which, apparently, sorted out those who were sophisticated and cultivated from those who were not. In fact, we all have a highly developed, complex and sensitive knowledge of grammar

Mental grammar – a MENTAL GRAMMAR. The hitch, of course, is that we are often not aware of the knowledge that we have, and also that we often don't have the words to express that knowledge. One aim of this unit is to help you solve this problem. However, it is true that grammatical change is more difficult to observe than, say, change in speech sounds. If you listen to older people or an old film, it's usually the pronunciation that is striking, not the grammar. We are less conscious of grammatical change (see also Exercise 2.2, p. 16).

One of the most important differences between OE and today's English is that in OE grammatical information was typically signalled by

Inflections the INFLECTIONS or endings of words. Today, there is one main inflection for nouns: a final *-s* (or *-es*) to signal number (e.g. *apple* vs. *apples*). Generally, if a noun has no *-s*, it is singular; if it has an *-s*, it is plural.

EXERCISE

7.1 Words borrowed from other languages can cause problems when it comes to deciding on how to make them plural or singular, because they do not take the regular English *-s* inflection. Are the following words plural or singular to you: *data, criteria, index, focus, formula*? How do you go about signalling a change from one to the other, or do you use the same form for both singular and plural? What about *octopus* – how would you make that plural?

If you look at Table 7.1, you'll see that there are six OE nouns listed in the top row: *hund* (= any dog, not just a hound), *deor* (= any animal, not just a deer), *cild* (= child), *oxa* (= ox), *fot* (= foot) and *lufu* (= love). Each noun carries a set of different inflections that make up a DECLENSION for that noun. I am giving them to you here so that you can appreciate how complex the inflections of nouns used to be, and so that I can explain some of the features of English we use today.

Declension

As you can see, these nouns vary according to number and according to CASE. What, you may wonder, are cases? In OE, nouns used to have inflections that indicated the function or relationship of words to other words in the sentence; that is to say, these nouns had case inflections. There were four main cases – NOMINATIVE, ACCUSATIVE, GENITIVE and DATIVE – each signalling different functions:

Case

Nominative
Accusative
Genitive
Dative

Case	Typical grammatical functions
Nominative	subject of the sentence (e.g. **Australia** beat England)
Accusative	direct object of a sentence (e.g. *Australia beat* **England**)
Genitive	possessor or part of a whole (e.g. **Jonathan's** book, each **of the students**)

Table 7.1 *Six noun declensions*

Singular	hound	deer	child	ox	foot	love
Nominative	hund	deor	cild	oxa	fot	lufu
Accusative	hund	deor	cild	oxan	fot	lufe
Genitive	hundes	deores	cildes	oxan	fotes	lufe
Dative	hunde	deore	cilde	oxan	fet	lufe
Plural						
Nominative/Accusative	hundas	deor	cildru	oxan	fet	lufa
Genitive	hunda	deora	cildra	oxena	fota	lufa
Dative	hundum	deorum	cildrum	oxum	fotum	lufum

(Based on Pyles, T. and Algeo, J. (4th edn) *The Origins and Development of the English Language*, Orlando, FL: Harcourt Brace Jovanovich, 1993: 110).

| Dative | indirect object (often recipient) or instrument (e.g. *I gave* the librarian *a book, I wrote* with a pen) |

An important point to note about today's English is that one can change grammatical functions simply by changing the word order. For example, by swapping the countries *England* and *Australia* I change what is the subject and what is the object. *Australia beat England* is not the same as *England beat Australia*. In OE, case inflections signal the grammatical roles of nouns in sentences, so in theory whatever I do to the word order there would still be one reading of the sentence. Consider the following made-up sentences:

1   Se guma syhð þone huntan   (nominative – verb – accusative)
    The man sees the hunter   (subject – verb – object)

2   Se hunta syhð þone guman   (nominative – verb – accusative)
    The hunter sees the man   (subject – verb – object)

3   Se guma þone huntan syhð   (nominative – accusative – verb)
    The man the hunter sees   (?? – ?? – verb)

The nouns *guma* and *hunta* follow the same pattern as the noun *oxa* in Table 7.1 (*guma*, incidentally, is the second element in the compound *bridegroom* = 'bride man'). The nominative form has a final *-a*, and the accusative has a final *-an*. Thus, in sentence (1), clearly the man is the subject (i.e. he is doing the seeing) and the hunter the object (i.e. he is being seen). In sentence (2), who is doing what changes, and so the inflections change too. (Note also that the word from which today's 'the' has developed changes its form according to case: *se*, if it is nominative, and *þone*, if it is accusative.) The important sentence is sentence (3). Here, it is clear in the OE version that it is the man (*guma*) who sees the hunter (*huntan*), but today's version – *the man the hunter sees* – could, in theory, be read both ways.

Today, we rely much more on word order to help us work out grammatical function. Usually, in statements the subject comes first, followed by the verb, and then the other parts of the sentence such as the object; thus, the 'normal' order is SVO. In practice it is likely that you would interpret sentence (3) as *the man* seeing *the hunter*, because the subject normally comes first. This pattern was also common in OE, but word order was generally more flexible. Let's take an example from Text 1 (Appendix IV) (I make no attempt to render the original handwriting here):

Erest weron bugend þises landes brittes
(first were inhabitants of this land Britons)
The first inhabitants of this land were Britons

Note that the verb 'were' occurs much earlier in the OE sentence than in the present-day translation. Today we would generally put the whole of the subject – 'the first inhabitants of this land' – before the verb. (Those of you who know Modern German will see an interesting similarity with this structure.) Another OE word-order pattern, where the object occurs before the verb, is well illustrated by the following fragment from the *Anglo-Saxon Chronicle* for the year 895 (objects are underlined; main verbs are emboldened):

7 þa burgware hie gefliemdon 7 hira monig hund ofslogon 7
(& then the townspeople <u>them</u> **put** to flight & <u>of them many hundreds</u> **slew** &)
& then the townspeople put them to flight & slew many hundreds of them &

hira scipu sumu genamon
(<u>of their ships some</u> **captured**)
captured some of their ships

This pattern hints at an important general change that has occurred in English grammar: it has shifted from an OV language (like today's Japanese) to a VO language (like today's English or French). The change has been in progress for thousands of years, and was well under way *before* English arrived in Britain. Moreover, it has gone hand-in-hand with the loss of case inflections, as given in Table 7.1. SVO languages generally lack case inflections, whereas SOV languages generally have them. One possible reason for this is that the verb in the SVO order makes a clear separation between subject and object: there is less potential for indeterminacy, and thus less need for a case marking to signal what an element is doing.

EXERCISES

7.2 (a) In case you are feeling confused, bear in mind that personal pronouns are almost as complex now as they were in OE, yet we use them without trouble. Like OE nouns, they are marked for case. Underline the pronouns in the examples below according to whether they are nominative (the subject), accusative (the object) or genitive (the possessor).

1 He sees him
2 Him he sees
3 He sees his face

(b) Second-person pronouns used to be more marked for case and number than they are now. If you compare Table 7.2 for ME and Table 7.3 for today's English, you'll see that *you* has become the predominant form.

Table 7.2 *Second-person pronouns in Middle English*

Grammatical function	Singular	Plural
Subjective (nominative)	Thou	Ye
Objective (accusative)	Thee	You
Possessive (genitive)	Thy/thine	Your/yours

Table 7.3 *Second-person pronouns in today's English*

Grammatical function	Singular	Plural
Subjective (nominative)	You	You
Objective (accusative)	You	You
Possessive (genitive)	Your/yours	Your/yours

The EMod.E period was one of transition with a mixture of *you* forms and *thou* forms. Interestingly, the factors that determined the usage of second-person pronouns in this period were not simply grammatical. The situation was somewhat like that in today's French (*tu* and *vous*) or German (*Sie* and *du*). *You* became a prestige form associated with the upper classes, whereas the opposite happened for *thou*. Thus, to an extent, the usage of the terms was **Sociolinguistic** SOCIOLINGUISTIC – language usage correlated with social groups. But speakers increasingly exploited these associations: for example, *you* could be used to express politeness, whereas *thou* could be used **Pragmatic** to express condescension. Thus, usage was also PRAGMATIC – language usage interacted with the context to create a range of meanings. Look carefully at the usage of second-person pronouns in Text 5 (Appendix IV). What is determining their usage? (*Hint:* Start by considering whether they follow the grammatical pattern given in Tables 7.2 and 7.3.) Can you explain why the second-person pronouns in Text 6 are governed by different principles?

What legacy did these noun inflections leave today's English? To begin with, I shall be referring closely to the noun declensions in Table 7.1 (p. 59). Today's plural marker – the final *-s* – survives from the *-as* nominative/accusative plural form, as exemplified by *hundas*. In OE there were other types of nouns with different plurals. Over time speakers and writers extended the *-s* plural marker across most nouns. However, some of the other types of plural marking have survived and this has led to some variability today. *Deor*, to the right of *hundas*, has zero marking for plurality. This has survived today. It would sound awkward, if you spoke about 'deers'. *Sheep* also belongs to this noun declension, as did a lot of other nouns that have now been taken over by the *-s* plural.

Cild, the next declension, has an interesting plural. In OE the plural was *cildru*. This form developed into *childer*. Have you heard the word *childer*? If you live in the north of England, it is possible that you have heard it. The *-n* of *children* was not present in OE. *Children* acquired a second plural ending, the *-n* that is used in the noun declension to the right exemplified by *oxan*. *Brethren* has a similar history. The use of *-n* as plural ending used to be popular. In the EMod.E period one often finds examples such as *eyen, shoen, housen, treen*, and the first two of these might still be heard in Scottish English. Now, in the majority of dialects, they all take the *-s* plural ending. The only pure survivor of this declension is *oxen*.

The following declension, exemplified by *fot*, is characterised by the fact that it not only had inflections but also changed the vowel of its basic form. Today, that vowel change *foot/feet* is a mark of the plural, but in OE note that it is also found in the dative singular and that not all plural forms had it. Only later did it become a distinctive marker of plurality. It survives in words such as *feet, geese, teeth, mice, lice* and *men*. As far as the final declension is concerned, it has no interesting survivals in terms of plurality, so let's move on to consider case.

I've already touched on the idea that other means, such as word order, are now being used to express some of the grammatical functions formerly achieved with case. The case that merits our particular attention is the genitive case, since it is from this that we get the apostrophe-*s*. If you look at Table 7.1, you will see that the most common genitive singular marker was the *-es* inflection. We saw an example of it quoted from Text 1 (in Appendix IV). Where today we would use the preposition *of* to indicate the relationship between the 'inhabitants' (*bugend*) and 'this land', thus giving 'inhabitants of this land', in OE they would use the genitive inflection *-es*, thus giving *bugend þises landes*. Generally, prepositions such as *of* were used less in OE. This particular genitive inflection, the *-es*, gave rise to the apostrophe-*s* that we use today. It was extended to other nouns, just as the *-as* plural inflection was extended to nouns that originally marked the plural in other ways. In fact, these two inflections merged: by ME both were written *-es*. So, for example, OE *hundes* (genitive singular) and OE *hundas* (the plural) both became ME *houndes*. During ME virtually all nouns were reduced to two forms: one without *-es* to indicate a singular, and one with *-es* to indicate either a genitive singular or a plural. Most other inflections had died out.

Middle English	Grammatical function	Today's English	Grammatical function
hound(e)	singular	*hound*	singular
hound(e)s	genitive singular	*hound's*	genitive singular
hound(e)s	plural	*hounds*	plural
hound(e)s	genitive plural	*hounds'*	genitive plural

This situation is in fact not so very different from that of today. In *speech*, there are also two forms: *hound* has one form without [z] at the end and one with. The idea of using a *written* apostrophe before the <s> to identify a genitive singular was not adopted until the seventeenth century, and the idea of using it after the <s> to identify a genitive plural was not adopted until the eighteenth century. Today, there is a lot of confusion in actual usage.

EXERCISES

7.3   Look through the texts in the 'mini-corpus' (Appendix IV) and try to find examples of the genitive marked with an *-es* inflection (i.e. nouns to which we would today add an apostophe–*s*). Be careful not to confuse it with something acting purely as a plural marker.

7.4   Investigate the confusion today about the usage of the apostrophe-*s*. Collect examples of incorrect usage. You are more likely to find them in informal writing. As well as collecting various nouns with the apostrophe-*s*, watch out for that notorious problem: confusion between *its* (= the genitive) and *it's* (= a contraction of *it is*). Does your collection of examples provide evidence that the use of the apostrophe-*s* may be changing?

In this unit, you will have noticed that in terms of inflections English has become a lot less complex. When we look at verbs in the next unit, we will see a very similar situation, and, in that unit, I will also comment on why English has lost much of its inflectional complexity. You will also have noticed that over time English has come to rely more heavily on word order (and prepositions) to do the job inflections once did. English has moved from being an INFLECTIONAL LANGUAGE like Latin or Arabic towards being what is known as an ISOLATING LANGUAGE like

Inflectional language

Isolating language

Chinese or Vietnamese, relying much more – though not completely – on word order to signal grammatical information.

EXERCISES

7.5 The *s*-genitive (the apostrophe-*s*) does not now behave in quite the same way as an inflection. In OE the *s*-genitive was an inflection used to indicate the function of the individual words to which it was fixed. In Mod.E it has become a grammatical particle that can be freely moved around, and can signal the function of a whole phrase. Thus, in the phrase *the head of department's office* the head of the phrase is *head* (the person who possesses the office), but the apostrophe-*s* is appended to the last word of the phrase *department*. When the *s*-genitive refers to a group of words it is called, sensibly enough, a GROUP GENITIVE. What is the longest group genitive you can devise?

Group genitive

DISCUSSION POINT

Although we cannot predict changes with certainty, how much further would you guess this process of inflectional simplification will go? Can we get rid of irregular plurals (e.g. *feet*, *children*) or non-native plurals (e.g. *criteria*, *indices*)? Can we get rid of the apostrophe-*s*? Are there varieties of English where this happens already? If English is made completely regular, what will be the advantages and for whom?

SUMMARY

- The most dramatic change in English grammar has been the loss of inflections. English has moved from being an inflectional language towards being an isolating language.
- The inflectional complexity of the past has its legacy in irregular plurals (e.g. *sheep*) and in the apostrophe-*s* of written English.
- Today, there is much confusion over the usage of the apostrophe-*s*.
- Today, personal pronouns are almost as complex as they were in OE. Second-person pronouns used to be more complex, and in the EMod.E period were used to signal social and pragmatic information.

FOLLOW-UP READING

Dick Leith's *A Social History of English* (London: Routledge, 1997) contains a readable general overview of the history of English grammar. However, you will need more detail. You could try David Crystal's *Encyclopedia of the English Language* (Cambridge: Cambridge University Press, 2003), pp. 20–1 (OE grammar), 44–5 (ME grammar), 70–1 (EMod.E grammar), and also 200–3 for some relevant pages on number and the *s*-genitive. Alternatively, you can look up the sections on nouns in a standard historical textbook. Much of this unit has focused on OE because grammar changes relatively slowly, and so we need to compare distant periods in order to see clear contrasts. The best introductory textbook on OE is Peter Baker's *Introduction to Old English* (Oxford: Blackwell, 2003). Tony Jebson's web pages at http://lonestar.texas.net/~jebbo/learn-OE/contents.htm offer a good overview of OE grammar. For other OE internet resources, see Cathy Ball's OE pages at http://www.georgetown.edu/faculty/ballc/OE/old_english.html.

GRAMMAR II

Verbs

8

As with nouns, verbs have experienced a dramatic loss of inflectional complexity. This has been counterbalanced by a rise in the use of auxiliary verbs.

Why is it that to form the past tense of the verb *walk* we add *-ed*, whereas to form the past of the verb *drink* we change the vowel so that we get *drank*? This is one of a number of present-day irregularities in English that can be explained by looking at its development. As with nouns, we need to look at how verbs signal their grammatical function, and how this has changed over time.

EXERCISE

8.1 In inflectional terms, present-day English regular verbs are very simple. Take the base or root form of a regular verb (e.g. *walk*). How many different inflections can you put on the end of it? Now, try to work out the grammatical function of each of these inflections (it may help if you devise short sentences to test the verb form).

Table 8.1 gives an idea of how present-tense verb inflections have changed from OE to the present day (all inflections occur after the letter <r>). Where alternative forms exist, they are given in parentheses.

Table 8.1 *OE present tense verb inflections*

Number	Person	Today	EMod.E	ME (Midlands)	OE (West Saxon)
Singular	1st I	hear	hear	here	hiere
	2nd you	hear	hearest	her(e)st	hierst
	3rd he/she/it	hears	heareth (-s)	her(e)þ (-es)	hierþ
Plural	1st we	hear	hear	heren (-es)	hieraþ
	2nd you	hear	hear	heren (-es)	hieraþ
	3rd they	hear	hear	heren (-es)	hieraþ

Regularisation

An important point to note is that – as with nouns – the general process over time has been one of REGULARISATION, with the gradual erosion of inflectional complexity. The situation used to be even more complicated than Table 8.1 suggests, because there was also a set of inflections for the past tense. Let's start by focusing on the one remaining inflection for person in today's English, the -s of the third person singular. In fact, in some varieties of today's English – some dialects of East Anglia, for example – even this inflection has been lost. If you look down the line to the far right, you'll see that in OE (the West Saxon dialect) there was no -s, but instead an *(e)*þ. (Remember that the character 'thorn' <þ> was later replaced by *th*.) In ME we get both forms. Note that here I am representing the Midlands dialect. (Chaucer wrote in what was essentially the East Midlands dialect.) Differences between dialects in earlier periods were much greater than now, as we shall see in the next unit, and, moreover, there was no 'standard' written form that I can choose to represent in the table. Why did the -s suddenly appear as an option in the ME Midlands dialect? The Scandinavians who settled in the north and east had provided English with the -s inflection. Over time this spread southwards through the rest of the country. By the EMod.E period, the *-eth* inflection was in serious decline, and came to be seen as rather archaic (in fact, there is some evidence to suggest that, even when *-eth* was written in EMod.E, it was pronounced like the -s inflection). It survived longest in the words *hath* and *doth*, which are still found in the eighteenth century.

EXERCISE

8.2 Note examples of *-eth* or -s in the 'mini-corpus' in Appendix IV. In particular, can you explain why Text 6, the Authorised Version of the Bible, is dominated by *-eth*?

Let's turn to tense. We noted earlier that the regular way of forming the past tense in English is simply to add the inflection *-ed*. However, there are a number of irregular verbs. English, in common with other Germanic languages, divides its verbs into two groups – so-called weak and strong – according to how they form their past tense and past participle. (If you are not clear about what a past participle is, make sure that you have read the description given in the answer to Exercise 8.1.)

Weak verbs add a *-d* or *-t* to the root in order to form the past or the past participle, for example:

Present	Past	Past participle
kiss	kissed	kissed
fill	filled	filled
build	built	built
hear	heard	heard

The vast majority of verbs in English form their past and past participles in this way.

Strong verbs do not add an inflection, but change the vowel of their base form:

Present	Past	Past participle
ride	rode	ridden
speak	spoke	spoken
see	saw	seen
drink	drank	drunk

All strong-verb past participles originally had the inflection *-en* at the end and also *ge-* at the beginning. So, in OE the past participle of the verb *ride* is *geriden*.

EXERCISE

8.3 Old forms of participles have survived in some contexts. Where might you hear:

> *drunken* as opposed to *drunk*
> *molten* as opposed to *melted*
> *stricken* as opposed to *struck*
> *shrunken* as opposed to *shrunk*

One should bear in mind here that not all speakers of English make the same distinctions between the past and past participle; some use one form for both. Thus, today many speakers of English use *done* as both past participle (*It was done well*) and simple past (*She done well*), and many are using *drunk* for the simple past (e.g. *She drunk the milk*). Variations such as these or those of the previous unit are part and parcel of gradual language change: before a change is completely regular there will be variation with the new and the old forms that are still part of the system.

The most important change to these weak and strong verb patterns is the conversion of the minority of strong verbs to the weak pattern. According to one estimate, five-sixths of the 360 or so strong verbs have changed. At various points in time, you can find both strong and weak forms of a verb. Thus, in the sixteenth century you can find both *laughed – low, crept – crope* and *helped – holp*.

EXERCISE

8.4 Which of the following pairs would you use: *dived – dove, hanged – hung, weaved – wove, strived – strove, digged – dug*? Would you use both but in different contexts? Your response will probably depend on factors such as your variety of English, or the specific meaning you wish to convey. Interestingly – bizarrely, perhaps – sometimes the item in a pair given above that is more frequently used is not following the regular 'add *-ed*' pattern.

It's worth noting that all new verbs follow the *-ed* weak pattern. In other words, if we want to indicate the past tense or make a participle, we put an *-ed* on the end of the word. For example, a British television advertisement for the soft drink *Tango* converts the brand name into a verb and makes it a past participle by adding *-ed*: *You know when you've been tangoed*. Extending a pattern in this way, just as happens with the extension of the English *-s* plural inflection to etymologically foreign **Analogy** words, is change by ANALOGY: a process whereby one part of the language is remodelled according to the pattern of another part. This process is involved in many language changes.

Auxiliary verbs Let's turn to AUXILIARY VERBS. What are auxiliary verbs? I will intro-
Main verbs duce a distinction between MAIN VERBS and auxiliary verbs by way of some examples:

1   I *may* drive
2   I *do* not drive
3   It *is being* driven
     It *has been being* driven

In each case the main verb is *drive*. The italicised auxiliary verbs help the main verb in some particular way; they perform functions that in other languages might be performed by inflections. I'm going to focus mainly on the use of *do* as an auxiliary verb, as illustrated in example (2). However, a general point to note about auxiliary verbs is that the further you go back in time the less likely you are to find a series of auxiliary verbs. In fact, neither of the examples in (3) above existed in EMod.E, and the final (admittedly rare) example *It **has been being** driven* is a twentieth-century development.

First, a brief comment on the verb in example (1) above. *May* is a MODAL VERB. Modal verbs are a subset of auxiliary verbs and include: *may, can, will, shall* and *must*. But they used not to be fully-fledged auxiliary verbs – they could stand alone. Sentences like *I must away* or *The truth will out* sound archaic (Shakespearean?), because they reflect the modal usage of earlier periods of English. Modern equivalents would be something like *I must go away* and *The truth will come out*, where a main verb is included. Today, the modals do not take inflections or express tense. But again this used not to be the case. *May, can, will* and *shall* used to have the past tense equivalents *might, could, would* and *should*. Now, the difference between, say, *may* and *might* is primarily a matter of meaning. If you say *Might I go* as opposed to *May I go*, the difference is to do with increased tentativeness, not reference to the past. The meanings of the modals have also changed (in accordance with Traugott's hypotheses about the direction of semantic change discussed in Unit 6).

Modal verb

Today, the meanings typically expressed by the modals are:

permission, possibility, ability = *can, could, may, might*
obligation, necessity = *must, should, need to, ought to*
volition (i.e. intention), prediction = *will, would, shall, be going to*

All the modals used to express rather different meanings. In OE, *shall* generally expressed obligation. This sense does occur occasionally today, but sounds somewhat archaic or is part of a register characterised by archaisms (e.g. the biblical Ten Commandments: 'Thou shalt not . . .'). Nowadays, in sentences like *I shall discuss dialects in the next unit* or *You shall finish this unit soon*, the meanings are to do with intentions and predictions, not obligation (note that, in accordance with Traugott, intention and prediction are more self-orientated than obligation, which can rely on some external authority).

EXERCISE

8.5 In the light of the discussion in the above paragraphs, investigate the modals 'shall' and 'can', referring in particular to Text 5 from 1567. Can they stand alone? Do they carry inflections? Has the meaning changed?

The development of the auxiliary verb *do* represents one of the most important changes in the English language. Today, it can be used as an auxiliary in a variety of ways: for emphasis in statements (e.g. *They do look for trouble*), to form a negative statement (e.g. *They do not look for trouble*), and in questions (e.g. *Do they look for trouble?*). In OE the use of *do* was somewhat different. As a main verb, it seems to have originally meant 'to put or place something somewhere': 'ðæt mon his sweord *doo* ofer his hype' (King Ælfred, *Gregory's Past*, 897) (= literally, that man his sword places over his hip). Indeed, *do* can still be used as a main verb today with the sense of 'putting', 'giving' or 'performing'. Consider: *to do to death, to do someone credit, to do some work*. It was not until ME that it developed as a common auxiliary.

From Late ME until about 1700, *do* was popular as a 'dummy' auxiliary, that is to say, an auxiliary that is relatively empty of meaning. Examples can be seen in Text 7 (Appendix IV) (John Milton, 1644): *For Books are not absolutely dead things, but **doe contain** a potencie of life in them to be as active as that soule was whose progeny they are; nay they **do preserve** as in a violl the purest efficacie.*... The historical meanings of *do* are often a pragmatic matter; they are used to express particular meanings in context. Note that Milton uses *do* in both instances above to help express a contrast (*but **doe contain**; nay they **do preserve**). Do could help manage the discourse or add to its intensity. The important point to note here is that *do* does not always simply add emphasis as it does today. Consider this text: 'when thou lokeste on the hearbes and trees, howe they **do growe**, and flowryshe in places, convenient for them [...]. For some of them **do growe** and sprynge in the feldes, other in the mountaynes, other in the marish, and other **do cleue** to the rocks [...] (George Colville, *Boethius' Consolation of Philosophy*, 1556). There is no emphasis of the type we would expect today. If you interpret every instance of *do* in Shakespeare as adding emphasis, you will be misreading Shakespeare, particularly as Shakespeare and other literary writers often used *do* if they needed an extra syllable to make up a metrical line.

The typical way of forming questions in OE had been to reverse the normal subject–verb order. This question-forming method was still regularly used in EMod.E. Thus, Shakespeare could write 'Spake you of Caesar?' (*Antony and Cleopatra* III.ii.11), reversing the normal order for a statement: *You* (subject) *spake* (verb) *of Caesar*. But by Shakespeare's time questions were being formed simply by placing *do* before the subject: 'Do you see this?' (*Hamlet* IV.v.197).

The typical way of forming negative statements in OE was by supplying the word *ne* (usually before the verb): 'he *ne* iaf him al' (*Peterborough Chronicle*, 1140) (= he did not give him all). They could also be formed by adding *ne* before the verb (auxiliary or main) and *not* after: '*Ne* con ic *noht* singan' (King Ælfred, Cædmon's *Hymn*, ninth century) (= I know not [how] to sing). In sentences like this, *not* added emphasis. Note here that what we are saying is that multiple negation (e.g. 'We don't need no education') was a regular feature of English and served the useful function of emphasis. Only later, as we shall see in the following unit, did such grammatical constructions become a focus of attention for prescriptivists. By EMod.E, *ne* is virtually obsolete, leaving just *not*: 'she vnderstode hym not' (Text 3, Caxton, 1490). This method of forming negative statements carries on well into the EMod.E period. But at this time we also find *do* beginning to be used with increasing frequency. So, in John Bunyan's *The Pilgrim's Progress* (1678) we can read both 'I care not what I meet' and 'I did not put the question to thee.' (Check Text 6(a) for examples of negative statements formed without *do*. The fact that the *do* construction is absent from a 1611 text can be explained again by the fact that it is a religious text representing the language of earlier periods.) Note that in the new *do* construction the position of *not* has changed, so that it comes before the main verb (*I care not* vs. *I did not put*).

In this and the last unit, we have seen some radical changes in inflections of words. But why did English lose its inflectional complexity? (Refer back to the possible reasons for language change given towards the end of Unit 2.) One convincing explanation concerns a structural change elsewhere in the language system. English underwent a phonological change leading to a grammatical change: the inflections at the ends of many words had ceased to be stressed, and were thus liable to blend with other inflections and disappear altogether, since people could not hear them so well. Evidence for this is in the considerable spelling variation for inflections. The neat Tables 7.1 and 8.1 are idealised paradigms, disguising all the messiness of actual practice. Another explanation points out that British English has experienced contact with an array of different languages (i.e. Celtic, Norse and French), and there may well have been some pressure for regularisation, in order to make it easier for people to communicate. Outside Britain, English – as we shall see in Unit 11 – has come into contact with many languages, creating yet further pressure to regularise the inflectional system.

DISCUSSION POINT

Note that, as in the example from King Ælfred above, a regular way of forming a negative statement in the past has been to use more than one negative word. In what varieties of today's English are you more likely to meet double or multiple negatives? What are the social implications of using double or multiple negatives? Is there any *linguistic* reason why they are a problem (consider whether communication is impaired or made more effective)?

SUMMARY

- Today, there is one remaining inflection for person, the *-s*, which is a Scandinavian borrowing. The Anglo-Saxon inflection used in OE, the *-eth*, lingered on until the eighteenth century.
- The presence today of a number of verbs that form their past and past participles in an irregular way (i.e. not with an *-ed* inflection) can be explained by examining the development of weak verbs and strong verbs. The strong-verb pattern has become increasingly rare. In a few cases, a verb has both strong and weak forms (e.g. *hung – hanged*).
- Auxiliary verbs have played an increasingly important role in English. Today, it is not unusual to have two or more auxiliary verbs in a row.
- A subset of auxiliary verbs, the modal verbs, have undergone dramatic change, both in terms of their grammatical characteristics and their meanings.
- The auxiliary *do* has had a profound effect on the development of English grammar, playing a role in forming emphatic statements, questions and negative statements.
- Two explanations, one structural and the other sociolinguistic, have been put forward for the dramatic loss of inflectional complexity in English: (1) the loss of distinctiveness in pronunciation, due to the fact that the inflections were unstressed; and (2) the regularisation of inflections to facilitate communication between peoples speaking different languages and dialects. There is good evidence in spelling for the first of these.

FOLLOW-UP READING

The same readings mentioned in the last unit from Dick Leith's *A Social History of English* (London: Routledge, 1997) and David Crystal's

Encyclopedia of the English Language (Cambridge: Cambridge University Press, 2003) are also relevant to this unit. In addition, pp. 204–5 and 212 in Crystal's *Encyclopedia* contain relevant general information on verbs, and, of course, you can look up the sections on verbs in a standard historical textbook. For a clear description of the general grammatical characteristics of each period of English, try Jeremy Smith's *Essentials of Early English* (London: Routledge, 1999). The readings and websites on OE suggested in the previous unit are relevant too.

9 DIALECTS IN BRITISH ENGLISH

> Dialects in Britain can be explained with reference to the presence and movement of various peoples, as well as the fact that language change took place at different speeds for different groups.

Twenty years ago I arrived in the city of Lancaster in the north-west of England, having travelled up from London, where I was born and bred. Now, the speech of most of the north-west is fairly familiar to me, but at the time I was struck by what I heard. The word *book* sounded like [buːk], not [bʊk]. People would tell me that they wanted something *fixing*, rather than that they wanted something *fixed*. And where was I going, if I went up a *ginnel*? (A *ginnel* turned out to be a narrow passageway between buildings.) What I was experiencing was a different

Dialect   DIALECT, a different regional dialect. The term dialect refers to a variety of language characterised in terms of pronunciation, grammar and lexis;

Accent   the term ACCENT refers to a variety of language characterised in terms of pronunciation only.

EXERCISES

9.1   Can you think of features of your dialect that make it distinctive, features that contrast with the features of dialects in other places? Try to find features at each linguistic level: grammatical, lexical and phonological (i.e. pronunciation). So, for example, for English dialects, someone who says *he say it* (as opposed to *he says it*) may well come from Norfolk; someone who says *bairn* (as opposed to *child*) may well come from the far north of England or Scotland; and someone who pronounces the word *singer* as [sɪŋɡə] (as opposed to [sɪŋə]) may well come from west central England (e.g. Birmingham, Manchester, Liverpool).

9.2 Become familiar with some of the varieties of English accents, by exploring the recordings at: http://www.bbc.co.uk/ voices/ (or the other internet sound archives mentioned in Appendix VI). You could, for example, listen to some of the varieties I have just mentioned in the previous exercise.

If you go back in time, the regional differences between dialects and accents were even more dramatic. It is not difficult to suggest some of the reasons why this is so. Before the nineteenth century travel for the bulk of the population consisted of walking, and thus most people lived and died without venturing much further than a few miles from their home. Britain was sparsely populated. It had perhaps 1 million inhabitants around the time of the Norman conquest. And before late EMod.E, there was no 'national' media. What all this means is that different varieties of English developed relatively independently of each other, as people generally did not come into contact with each other. These differences were increased by the fact that different things happened to different parts of the country. Let's start by considering the arrival of English in Britain.

You will remember from Unit 1 that various Germanic tribes – the Angles, the Saxons and the Jutes – began to settle in Britain in the fifth century. Though it is controversial as to whether there were any real differences between these tribes, the placename evidence hints at different patterns of settlement (cf. Unit 1), and it is linguistically improbable that these diverse groups of settlers were all speaking exactly the same variety. Some of the dialectal differences in today's English may originate in the Germanic dialects spoken by these tribes, though firm evidence is lacking. Map 9.1 shows the traditional view of what are believed to be the OE dialect areas. As you can see, there are four main dialects: (1) *Northumbrian* – north of the Humber and south-east Scotland; (2) *Mercian* or *Midland* – further to the south and containing two main sub-dialects, West Midland and East Midland; (3) *Kentish* – the south-east (including modern Kent and Surrey); and (4) *West Saxon* – south of the Thames, from Sussex to Devon, but excluding the Cornish-speaking area. Sometimes Northumbrian and Mercian are grouped together as *Anglian*. These are rather generalised dialect areas in the sense that sub-groupings can be distinguished within them. Mercian texts, in particular, show wide variation (hence, it is especially useful to make further subdivisions here). Also, the boundaries are approximate: there is insufficient evidence to be precise.

Some of the OE dialect boundaries seem to coincide with today's dialect boundaries. In Exercise 9.1, I mentioned that someone who pronounces the word *singer* as [sɪŋgə], as opposed to [sɪŋə], may well come from west central England (e.g. Birmingham, Manchester, Liverpool). As it happens, this is a pretty good match for the Mercian dialect area, specifically, the West Midland sub-dialect. Today, an import-

Map 9.1
Old English
dialect areas

ant boundary for traditional rural accents is that between Northumbrian and Mercian. Below a line roughly from the mouth of the river Humber to the mouth of the river Lune near Lancaster, you can find, for example, *ground* pronounced [grɒʊnd], *blind* pronounced [blaɪnd] and *wrong* pronounced [rɒŋ]. However, above that line, although they are now very rare, it is still possible to find them pronounced [grʊnd], [blɪnd] and [raŋ].

In Unit 1, we have seen how the Scandinavians invaded and settled in the north and east of England during the OE period, and how the Scandinavian languages, Old Norse and Old Danish, influenced placenames in those regions. Although the Scandinavian languages and English were not distantly related (see the Indo-European family tree in Appendix II) and were to a degree mutually comprehensible, their presence in Britain sharpened the distinction between northern and southern varieties of English. Do you remember Caxton's 'eggs' story in Text 3 (Appendix IV)? The communication problem can be explained by noting that *egges* is a Norse loanword, and *eyren* is an Anglo-Saxon OE word. At the time the story takes place, in the fifteenth century, *egges* had worked its way down and was well established in London, but further south in Kent *eyren* was still current.

EXERCISE

9.3 All of the words given below are typically found in the north of England. Use an etymological dictionary to find out the etymology of these words, noting down the language from which they are borrowed. It will also be interesting to note down COGNATE forms (i.e. other forms in the same language family branch), if they are listed, in today's Scandinavian languages (e.g. Danish, Norwegian, Swedish). Present your results in a table, so that by looking across a row you can get a sense of how similar these northern dialectal words are to those in Scandinavian languages.

Cognate

garth	(yard)	laik	(to play)
kist	(chest)	tarn	(small mountain lake)
nay	(no)	kirk	(church)
steg	(gander)	nieve	(fist)
smoot	(narrow passage)	fell	(hill, mountain)
beck	(brook)	addle	(to acquire)

As we have already noted during the course of this book, the ME period was one of variety, including great regional variety. Let's not forget that a number of languages were used in Britain at this time: Latin was used for formal texts (e.g. laws, religious texts, scholarly works), Norman French was used for administration and spoken by the upper ranks, while English became a set of largely spoken dialects, except in Cornwall, Wales and Scotland, where Celtic languages were spoken. As Map 9.2 shows, the ME dialect areas were very similar to those of OE. There is no one principal dialect in ME. In fact, important ME texts survive in all five dialects. That is because there was no generally accepted

Map 9.2
Middle English
dialect areas

written standard. As we saw in Unit 3, if people wrote in English, they generally wrote as they would speak, so they would reproduce their particular accent and dialect.

EXERCISE

9.4 Reconsider Exercise 3.2 (p. 23), and in particular scrutinise the variant spellings of *sword*. There may be one that suggests a particular accent to you (*Hint:* look at the first letter.) Similarly, check the entry for *father* in an etymological dictionary.

The discussion above has paid attention to different settlement patterns and differences in contact with other languages (e.g. Norse). But this is only part of the story of English dialects. Variation also comes about when the dialectal features of different speakers develop in different ways (or not at all). Let's look at accents in particular and reconsider the dramatic changes in long vowels that took place in EMod.E. You may remember that these changes were referred to as the 'Great Vowel Shift' (GVS) in Unit 3. (Turn back and reread the relevant paragraphs now, pp. 28–30.) Not every variety has experienced the full course of change referred to as the GVS, and some have undergone notable developments after the period of the GVS. Take as an example the pronunciation of the word *house*. The chart below suggests how the pronunciation of *house* has changed over time. Practise the pronunciations given. (Check the symbols in Appendix III, so that you can get a sense of what sounds they represent.)

The changing pronunciation of 'house'

	OE	ME	EMod.E	Today?
house	huːs	huːs	haʊs	hɒʊs

The sound [uː] is already a high back vowel, so it can't be raised further, but instead develops into a diphthong [əʊ], and then [ɒʊ]. Has change stopped here? Let's consider popular London speech, specifically Cockney, which, in some respects, has undergone greater change than other accents. Here, the diphthong [ɒʊ] in words like *house* has developed yet further, losing the [ʊ] quality, so that pronunciations like [haːs] with more of a monophthong can be heard. (Strictly speaking, in Cockney speech the initial [h] would not be pronounced. This increases the potential for embarrassing ambiguities when one says something like 'You've got a big house'.)

EXERCISES

9.5 Have a guess at the exercises below. Don't panic if you feel that English dialects are something of a mystery. You can find some answers in Appendix V, where I will also suggest some recordings for you to listen to.

(a) Where in Britain has the pronunciation of the vowel [uː] in words such as *house* not undergone the GVS mapped out above?

(b) Where in Britain has the pronunciation of the vowels in words like *face* and *road* not followed the GVS and developed into diphthongs?

Post-vocalic

(c) Where in Britain can you still hear the <r> pronounced after a vowel in words like *car* and *farm* (this feature of people's speech is sometimes referred to as a 'burr')? Three hundred years ago POST-VOCALIC *r* was pronounced throughout England, but began to rapidly disappear in the south-east from the eighteenth century.

(d) Over the last few centuries, a new vowel sound [ʌ] in words such as *much*, *sun* and *money* has developed, particularly in the accent of speakers in the London region. Where in Britain is this vowel not used? What vowel is used instead in words such as those above?

(e) Over the last few centuries, the vowel sound [a] in words such as *bath*, *grass* and *dance* has changed to [ɒː], particularly in the accent of speakers in the London region. Where in Britain has this change not taken place?

(f) In Unit 7 we looked at the use of second-person pronouns and, in particular, the use of *you* and *thou* forms in EMod.E. It is not the case, however, that *thou* forms have completely died out. Where in Britain can you still hear the *thou* forms of the second-person pronoun?

9.6 What do you think the areas you have identified in the above exercises in 9.5 have in common? Why is it that change has not occurred here and why has it occurred in other parts of Britain?

So far, we have been investigating the development of traditional rural dialects (excellent examples of these can be heard at http://collectbritain. co.uk/collections/dialects/). Traditional dialects tend to be frequently stereotyped. The south-western English dialect has been unfairly and often inaccurately caricatured on stage, since at least the time of Shakespeare (as you would have seen from Exercise 9.4 and its answer, those stereotypical south-western features of today used to extend right across the south of England, including Kent – they were features of a *southern* dialect). While these traditional dialects are still important, and are particularly apparent among older people in rural areas, we cannot ignore the effect of improved communications and of industrialisation, with its associated urbanisation, over the last 200 years or so. In fact, the frequent complaint today that 'dialects are dying out' reflects the fact that the basis for dialects has shifted. Nowadays, people regularly travel hundreds of miles and think nothing of it. People commute to work in London from as far afield as Birmingham. Such mobility would explain, for example, why 150 years ago there was a traditional Kentish dialect, while today it barely survives, such is the close and regular contact with London. Of course, this is not to say that traditional dialects are replaced by nothing. Relatively new dialect forms based on urban areas have become influential. There has been a mass exodus from rural areas into urban ones. This is dramatically illus- trated by these estimates of numbers of people living in rural communities in the late industrial period: 1851 – 50 per cent, 1891 – 28 per cent and 1911 – 22 per cent. So, instead of small relatively isolated communities where each person mingles with more or less the same people for a life-time, we have vast human melting-pots where people have diffuse social networks – mingling regularly with different people, adopting new speech forms and losing the old rural forms. Both developments in communication and the effects of urbanisation have contributed to DIALECT LEVELLING, a term referring to the loss of original traditional **Dialect levelling** dialectal distinctions.

Interestingly, the combination of communication networks and urban centres can have broader implications. Speech forms tend to spread out- wards from urban centres and particularly down lines of communication. The spread of London speech, something that has been happening for centuries, has recently attracted media attention, and the variety of English concerned has been given the jazzy title of 'Estuary English' (after the river Thames estuary). Evidence of Estuary English has been found in areas of Hull, Chester and Bristol – all of which have good communica- tion links with London. Features of Estuary English include the use of glottal stops (especially replacing [t] at the end of a word or before a con- sonant, e.g. *treatment*); the pronunciation of <l> in words like *hill*, so that it sounds more like [w]; and the pronunciation of the sound at the begin- ning of *Tuesday* so that it is [tʃuːzdeɪ] and not [tjuːzdeɪ].

DISCUSSION POINT

In everyday life people are as likely – or more likely – to make social judgements about regional dialects as they are to describe them, as this unit has attempted to do. What stereotypical characteristics are often attached to which dialect? If you are part of a group, try to come to an agreement about associations of various dialects. To help you, think about the use of dialects in plays or films: which dialects are used to create rustic, 'country bumpkin' characters, which for shifty, small-time gangsters, which for people in a position of power, which for the cuddly, cute characters, and which for the evil characters? You will probably be able to generate a fairly rich collection of associations for the dialects you choose. These are purely social judgements: there is no linguistic reason why one dialect suggests one thing and another something else. In fact, they are really judgements about the speakers of those accents, rather than the particular accent. What implications do such judgements have for, say, the selection of someone for a job, the treatment of children in a classroom or the election of someone for a government post?

SUMMARY

- Britain has considerable diversity in its accents and dialects, and this diversity begins with the arrival of the Angles, Saxons and Jutes speaking various Germanic dialects.
- OE is traditionally classified into four main dialect areas (Northumbrian, Mercian, Kentish and West Saxon), and these are very similar to those of ME. Today, some of these boundaries are still important dialectal boundaries.
- The settlement of the north and east of Britain by Scandinavians speaking Old Norse and Old Danish resulted in a sharpening of the distinction between northern and southern varieties of English.
- The fact that accents and dialects developed in different ways (or not at all) resulted in further variation. For example, not all accents experienced the full set of changes comprising the Great Vowel Shift.
- More recently, urban dialects have become increasingly important, and these have tended to spread out along lines of communication.
- In a number of respects, London has been at the forefront of change.

FOLLOW-UP READING

The relevant pages on British English dialects and accents in David Crystal's *Encyclopedia of the English Language* (Cambridge: Cambridge University Press, 2003) are pp. 28–9, 50–1 and 324–7. Also, it's worth reading the pages on English in Scotland (pp. 328–33), Wales (pp. 334–5) and Ireland (pp. 336–7). For a historical perspective, the standard introductory book is Martyn F. Wakelin's *English Dialects: an Introduction* (London: Athlone Press, 1972). Clive Upton and J.D.A. Widdowson's *An Atlas of English Dialects* (Oxford: Oxford University Press, 1996; a paperback) is useful for particular features, and it contains some historical information. For a more comprehensive yet accessible treatment, with copious illustration, I would recommend Dennis Freeborn's *From Old English to Standard English* (London: Macmillan, 1998), particularly chapters 8–13. For present-day considerations of dialect, try Arthur Hughes and Peter Trudgill's *English Accents and Dialects* (3rd edn, London: Hodder Arnold, 1996). An excellent paper on dialect levelling, 1900–2000, by Paul Kerswill can be found at: http://www.universal teacher.org.uk/lang/rp.htm#8. If you are interested in 'Estuary English', the best collection of material is available on John Wells's web pages: http://www.phon.ucl.ac.uk/home/estuary/.

10 STANDARDISATION

The development of 'standard' English proceeded along very different lines for speech and writing, and thus they are considered separately here.

At the moment, my car needs two new tyres. The car itself was manufactured in Italy and the tyres in France. But I am confident that I could go down to my local garage in the north-west of England and be able to buy some suitable tyres. Why? Because tyres are manufactured throughout Europe, and in many other countries besides, according to a standard set of sizes. In fact, mass production, as in the automobile industry, relies on standardisation when it comes to assembling components from different suppliers: the bolts must be the right size for the holes in the chassis, the nuts must be threaded the right way for the bolts, the spanners must be the right size for the nuts, and so on. In this context, then, the notion of a standard is an agreed uniform set of sizes to which different manufacturers conform.

In *written* English too there is a certain standard: an agreed uniform set of forms to which different users conform. We do not normally spel werds enihau, make up snooky words or use structures grammatical strange, because this would make communication more difficult. But achieving communication can only be one factor in shaping the standard written English, since many different kinds of non-standard written (and spoken) language achieve communication. Standard written English attains greater uniformity by restricting the range of language choices, not just to those that achieve communication, but to a socially approved set. So, for example, in Unit 8 we saw that single or multiple negation were options in ME (e.g. using *ne*, *ne* plus *not*, or other combinations of negative elements), but in standard written English the only choice is single negation. STANDARDISATION, the process by which a standard is achieved, inhibits variation. Broadly speaking, the standardisation of written English gets under way early in the fifteenth century, is intense in the sixteenth, and trails off into the late seventeenth century, being more or less complete by the eighteenth. However, the more detailed picture shows that what gets standardised when depends on what part of the standard you are talking about. Regarding punctuation, for example, little standardisation took place before the second half of the seventeenth century. Also, sometimes the progress of standardisation is less than smooth, with people's usage of, for example, particular grammatical variants shifting towards the eventual standard, then receding and then going back to the standard.

Prior to the development of standard written English, there was much variation in writing. In the fifteenth century, William Caxton was keenly aware of this issue. In the *egges* story in Text 3 (Appendix IV), Caxton bewails the lack of an agreed standard in the ME period, and we have seen during the course of this book how variation occurred at every linguistic level. Rather like the automobile industry, Caxton's wish for some kind of standard had an economic dimension. Clearly, it would be very costly to print a different version of a book for every variety of English. So, Caxton needed to pick one variety of English that was widely understood and was socially valued (and thus would be taken seriously). Let us consider some possible choices.

John of Trevisa's translation of the *Polychronicon* (Text 2), completed in 1387, suggests one possible choice. He made the communicative argument that the dialects of the middle of England were more likely to be understood by people to either side – an argument for a Midlands dialect. Trevisa was alluding to what today's linguists would call a DIALECT CONTINUUM – the idea that there is a chain of dialects and accents, each differing a small amount from their neighbour, so that speakers can understand neighbouring dialects but have difficulty understanding dialects further away on the dialectal chain. But what about a dialect that was socially valued? London had the prestige of being the capital city, the political centre and the centre of commerce and administration. It was also by far the largest English city. The supremacy of the capital city was a uniquely English feature, one that was unrivalled in Europe. And what dialect were they speaking in London? In the late ME period – the period of importance in our discussion – London was a hybrid dialectal area. Remember that it sits on a kind of dialectal crossroads – the river Thames connects with East Anglia, the Midlands, Kent and the south-west. However, it is also important to note that London's commercial attention was directed primarily to the north, that it had good communications to the north and that it had also experienced significant immigration from that area. So, although geographically quite

Standardisation

Dialect continuum

far south in England and originally more a southern dialect, London by late ME is primarily a Midlands dialect (i.e. the dialect region to the north of London), with other elements mixed in.

There are further factors that explain why the main contributor to the written standard was the Midlands dialects and not the Southern. From the arrival of the Normans up until about 1430, all official documentation was written in French or Latin. During the fourteenth century, the prestige of French became somewhat reduced, at least among some sectors of the population, for political reasons: from 1337, England had been engaged in the so-called 'Hundred Years War' with France. Moreover, by the fifteenth century, the administrative system needed an efficient medium for communication, not a language understood by a very small elite. Around 1430, the Chancery or government scribes adopted a variety of English that was based on London, but with heavy Central Midlands influence, and this variety has been

Chancery Standard

called the CHANCERY STANDARD (some scholars have pointed out that the Chancery Standard mainly concerned spelling). The significance of this is that we now have an institution producing masses of paperwork in one variety of English that is then sent all over the country. Caxton set up his printing press in Westminster in 1476, close to the government offices. His adoption of a London-based variety of English, including some features of the English of official circles, was the obvious choice.

EXERCISE

10.1 It is a mistake to think that standard written English is centred on a southern variety of English. Moreover, the final written standard that emerges contains some important northern features, but lacks some important southern features. Take as an example today's third person plural pronouns *they*, *them* and *their*. These are descended from the northern forms, and are ultimately Scandinavian in origin. The equivalent southern forms were *hi*, *him* and *hire*.

(a) One of the most important inflections in standard written English was originally a northern form. What is it?

(b) Some core vocabulary items were originally northern words. Give some examples.

(*Hint:* Some answers to these questions are in Units 4 and 8. Think about features that are originally Scandinavian.)

The fact that printers like Caxton adopted a particular variety of English obviously did much to promote it, since they had the ability to mass produce it. But a recognised national standard of written English would most likely have come about even without printing, as is evidenced by the fact that the first stages of its development occurred before printing. Other factors were involved. Not only did the language of administration shift from a foreign language to English, but various prestigious domains of written language usage began to switch from Latin to English (Trevia's translation of the *Polychronicon*, Text 2, is an example of this). Scientific writing made this switch, beginning in the late fourteenth century and continuing into the seventeenth. Remember that one of the most prestigious domains of written language usage – religion – had been dominated by an entirely different language, namely Latin. A political move that led to change here was the Reformation: Henry VIII's split from the Roman Catholic Church in 1533. One way of challenging the power of the Catholic Church, which operated in Latin throughout Europe, was to produce texts in English. The first licensed English Bible appeared in 1537 and the Book of Common Prayer – a service book for the Church of England – in 1549. The most famous English Bible, promoted by James I, appeared in 1611. (You can see extracts from the 1611 Authorised Version of the Bible in Text 6.) All this had the effect of increasing a national focus on English. Moreover, it gave the kind of English that appeared in these 'serious' texts prestige.

What finally fixed the standard in the minds of users was the growth of dictionaries, grammar books, spelling books, and so on, particularly from the seventeenth century onwards. These were adopted in schools, and became arbiters of the language. They CODIFIED the standard by offering an authoritative consensus about what the standard consisted of. Moreover, especially in the second half of the eighteenth century, various individuals, such as Jonathan Swift, set themselves up as authorities on the English language and wrote books, often with the explicit aim of setting a standard variety of English in concrete. Many of these rules lack a sound basis: they reflect an appeal to pseudo-logic or to etymology, a wish to emulate the prestigious language Latin, or simply the whim of the writer.

Codified

EXERCISE

10.2 (a) Is it really possible to 'fix the language' to a certain standard, as many commentators in the eighteenth century wished to do?

(b) Below is a set of examples that would have troubled eighteenth or nineteenth century writers and are still hot issues today. What 'rule' is broken in each example and can you imagine why the 'rule' was devised?

1   Tom, ill upstairs, complained to his mother: 'What did you bring that book I didn't want to be read to out of up for?'

2   '... the voyages of the starship Enterprise, its continuing mission:
to explore strange new worlds,
to seek out new life and new civilisations,
to boldly go where no one has gone before.'

3   Share it among the two of you.

4   I never did nothing.

Today, we all consult authoritative sources, typically dictionaries, for word meanings, spellings, grammatical points, and so on. We've already seen the limitations of dictionaries in Unit 6. During the 'Discussion point' of Unit 2 (p. 19), I'm sure that many 'rules', perhaps learnt from past teachers, will have come to light. In fact, many of these rules can be traced back to the eighteenth century (a bonanza century for making rules) or earlier.

A final point to be made about standard written English is that it is not now recognisable as the Midlands dialect or, more importantly, as part of a dialect continuum. The processes of social approval and fixing mean that standard written English has not changed in the same way as other dialects. And some parts of standard English (e.g. intolerance of multiple negation), usually those derived from the prescriptivists, were never part of any dialect in the first place. Standard English is a *social* dialect not a regional one. Regional dialects have associated accents, but standard English can be spoken by speakers of any accent (nowadays, newsreaders on the BBC, speaking standard English, regularly have regional accents). And regional dialects and accents are normally arranged in chains, one shading into another, but standard English stands in contrast to all regional dialects.

So far, we've discussed the development of a written standard; we must now consider the possibility of a spoken standard. Can we today speak of a spoken 'standard'? Is there an accent – a variety of language characterised solely in terms of pronunciation – that matches the standard of written language? Is there an accent used by the vast majority of people and one that enjoys high prestige? Clearly, there is no one accent used by the majority of speakers. Even small groups of people are likely to have speakers of different accents. So, unlike the written standard, with speech there can be no notion of a uniform variety used by the majority. However, we can talk about a prestige form. I'm sure that most readers will have heard of the Queen's English, BBC English or simply 'talking posh'. Linguists sometimes refer to this accent as RECEIVED PRONUNCIATION (RP) ('received' has the earlier sense of 'accepted').

Received Pronunciation (RP)

For centuries, people have made aesthetic and social judgements about accents. (See, for example, Trevisa's comments on the Yorkshire accent in Text 2.) From the sixteenth century onwards, a growing number of writers designated the speech of the upper ranks and, in particular, of the court in London as a prestige form. For example, George Puttenham (1589) advises the poet to use 'the vsuall speach of the Court, and that of London and the shires about London within lx. myles, and not much aboue'. With royalty sited at London and a 60-mile radius including the important cultural centres Cambridge, Oxford and Canterbury, it is not a surprise that the prestige form was based here. In the nineteenth century, this form was firmly established as the accent of the ruling classes through the public-school system. Those who could afford to send their children to public schools did so in the expectation that they would experience the accent so strongly associated with the upper classes, in other words, Received Pronunciation. Scholars have argued that one effect of this was to break down the regional associations of RP: an RP speaker from the south would sound similar to an RP speaker from the north, because they had been through the same education system. Today, although the majority of RP speakers live in the south-east of England, it is the case that the non-localised nature of RP is one of its characteristics: if you hear an RP speaker, you may guess their social background, but not where they come from. This non-localised characteristic is one that RP shares with standard written English: both stand in contrast with regional accents/dialects. They are both social constructions.

Two other factors played a role in establishing the dominance of RP. Just as technology – the printing presses – had played a role in promoting a written standard, so technology was to play a role in promoting a particular accent. With the advent of radio broadcasting in the 1920s, the BBC needed to formulate a policy as to what variety of spoken English they would use, and they chose RP. The second factor was that RP was codified by British linguists in the twentieth century. It is the pronunciation given in dictionaries of English and taught to foreign learners of British English. More has been written about RP than any other accent. This is perhaps an odd state of affairs, if one considers that RP is a minority accent spoken today by around 3–5 per cent of the population of Britain.

Of course, the correlation of certain accents with certain classes is entirely a social matter. It has nothing to do with particular accents being linguistically better. However, this has not stopped people from evaluating others on the basis of the way they speak. RP, as well as the written standard, is sometimes used as a 'standard' for judging people, so that 'non-standard' is taken to mean deficient in some way. This everyday notion of 'standard' has no linguistic justification at all. For example, a commonly held idea is that non-RP speakers are 'lazy' or 'slovenly', because they don't pronounce all the letters in words. If you think about it, this idea doesn't match the facts. We saw in Unit 3 how *nobody* would pronounce all the letters in every word. In fluent speech, RP speakers, too, use reduced forms (e.g. no RP speaker would pronounce 'and' as [ænd], but much more likely [ən]) and 'drop letters' (e.g. the *t* in the phrase *soft pillow*). Indeed, there is no simplistic equation such that the more sounds we supply in pronouncing a word the higher up the social scale it will be rated. Consider the pronunciation of the word *sing*. The RP pronunciation is [sɪŋ]; a regional (west central England) pronunciation is [sɪŋg]. It is the regional pronunciation that has more sounds and more closely reflects the spelling of the word.

Today, RP has less authority than it used to have in the first half of the twentieth century. People still strongly associate it with high social status, but it does not have quite the prestige it once had. It is often referred to as 'plummy', 'stuck up' or 'contrived', and closely identifies a speaker with the establishment – something that might well be a nega-

Modified RP   tive feature, particularly for younger people. MODIFIED RP, a mixture of RP and regional features, is becoming more common. An interesting development has been the move by some RP speakers towards Estuary English. In fact, Estuary English has been described as lying in the middle of a scale with RP at one end and popular London speech at the other (or, as one newspaper put it, 'between Cockney and the Queen'). Thus, Nigel Kennedy, a violinist with an RP-speaking background, speaks Estuary English: a good vehicle for popularising classical music.

EXERCISES

10.3 What are the factors that lead to the standardisation of a particular accent or dialect?

10.4 (a) How helpful is the 'tyres' analogy with which I open this unit? In what ways might it be misleading or a distortion of the notion of 'standard' when applied to language?

(b) Many people, particularly politicians and the media, are notorious for their (wilful?) misunderstanding of the concept of 'standard' when it is applied to language. Part of the problem lies in an everyday usage of the word *standard*. Describe the nature of this misunderstanding, and the kind of abuse it can lead to.

10.5 In the past, the British royal family have been the stronghold of RP, but this seems to be changing. Younger members (e.g. Prince Andrew, Prince Edward) have distinctly different accents from the older members (e.g. the Queen, Prince Charles). Try to tape any news reports, interviews, speeches or documentaries involving members of the royal family. Then compare the speech of individuals, looking out, for example, for typical features of Estuary English (see the previous unit; also the Estuary English website listed there will supply a much more detailed description of Estuary English). An interesting extension of this study would be to compare old recordings of the royal family (e.g. the queen's coronation) with present-day recordings, and to note any changes that have occurred. (Remember that such old recordings are often available in public libraries.) The kind of features of conservative RP that you might listen out for include: *off* pronounced so that it rhymes with *awe* and not the vowel of *hot* (i.e. [ɔːf] and not [ɒf]); the vowel of *bat* pronounced so that it rhymes more closely with *bet* (i.e. [bɛt] and not [bæt]); and the second vowel of *refined* pronounced so that it rhymes more closely with *rained* than *rind* (i.e. [rəfeɪnd] and not [rəfaɪnd]).

DISCUSSION POINT

As far as language is concerned, what 'standard' should be taught in schools? Need a 'standard' be taught at all? In England this has been the subject of much debate. What should a teacher do, if a child writes a non-standard spelling? What should a teacher do, if a child uses non-standard grammar and lexis in writing? What should a teacher do, if a child uses a regional pronunciation? Consider also the possibility that there might be different solutions for different situations or different types of writing. If you are part of a group, you can set up a debate revolving around certain options.

SUMMARY

- The written standard begins to emerge in the early fifteenth century, primarily based on the Midlands dialect. Such a dialect was an effective medium for communication between north and south. It was also the major contributor to the dialect of the capital, with all the prestige that that entailed.
- The adoption of a London/Midlands variety for the administrative system and its uptake by printers like Caxton were important factors in promoting the written standard.
- The national focus on English was helped by the switch from French or Latin to English in various serious genres, notably religion. These genres fostered the developing standard with their prestige.
- From the seventeenth century onwards the standard was codified.
- A prestige accent based on the court and the London area emerges in the sixteenth century.
- The public-school system established RP as the dominant high-class accent. RP was promoted with the advent of broadcasting, and it was codified in the twentieth century. However, over the last few years RP has experienced something of a decline.
- The notion of 'standard' is very problematic. Clearly, the 'standard' in writing is different from the 'standard' in speech, and what the general public understand by 'standard' may yet be something else.

FOLLOW-UP READING

The relevant pages on standardisation in David Crystal's *Encyclopedia of the English Language* (Cambridge: Cambridge University Press, 2003) are pp. 54–5 on the written standard and p. 365 on RP. It is also worth reading pp. 110–11 and 113, where the notion of 'standard English' and of a 'world standard English' is considered (World Englishes will be the topic of the next unit). Some useful pages on 'traditional grammar', and in particular the prescriptive tradition, are pp. 78–9 and 192–6. In addition, most of the standard books on dialects (see the previous unit) or on the general history of the English language will include a section on the standardisation of English. Rather more advanced (though accessible) and cutting-edge is Laura Wright's collection of papers *The Development of Standard English, 1300–1800: Theories, Descriptions, Conflicts* (Cambridge: Cambridge University Press: 2000).

WORLD ENGLISHES

11

The crucial factor in the development of English over the last few centuries is its role in the world. English has been brought into contact with new environments and languages, and as a result has developed in new directions, giving rise to different varieties of English.

English has gone global. Today, English dominates the world stage in a number of language uses: it is the main language of publishing, science, technology, commerce, diplomacy, air-traffic control and popular music. The reasons for this are to do with the political and economic power of Britain in the nineteenth century and the United States in the twentieth century. These same reasons also account for a dramatic increase in the number of users of English. In the sixteenth century there were approximately 3 million speakers of English. Today, there are over 300 million native speakers of English. To this, one could add a further 300 million who regularly speak English as a second language (i.e. in addition to their native language), and then there are the countless numbers of people who have learnt English as a foreign language (more Chinese people are learning English than there are native speakers of English in the USA!). In fact, it has been estimated that in total around a billion people use English with varying degrees of proficiency. Calculating numbers of users of English is fraught with difficulties, but there can be no doubt that English is the most widely used language in the world.

EXERCISE

11.1 (a) List as many countries as you can where English is spoken as a native language (ENL countries).

(b) List as many countries as you can where English is spoken as a second language (ESL countries). Such countries usually give English some kind of official status; English may be used for administrative and legal purposes, or in certain newspapers; and often these countries were formerly part of the British Empire.

(c) List a selection of countries where English is spoken as a foreign language (EFL countries).

(d) Can you think of any problems with the above classification? Examples that do not fit the scheme?

World Englishes

With the international spread of English it is more appropriate now to speak of WORLD ENGLISHES. This term emphasises the fact that these varieties have developed out of their own unique set of circumstances and have their own identity. It is not appropriate to view them solely in relation to British standard written English. Many have developed their own 'standards', and some had no major input from British English (Philippines English, for example, has American English as the major input). North American and British English are the two most important national varieties, in terms both of numbers of speakers and of world-wide impact (Britain through its former Empire, and North America through its economic power), and so I shall focus on these.

EXERCISE

11.2 Let's tackle a British myth. Prince Charles, as reported in *The Times* (1995), made the following comments on American English: 'very corrupting'; 'people tend to invent all sorts of nouns and verbs and make words that shouldn't be'; '[w]e must act now to insure that English – and that, to my way of thinking, means English English – maintains its position as the world language well into the next century'. The idea that American English is 'corrupting' English English is a common refrain. Let me try an experiment on you British readers. All of the following words are currently used in British English. Which of them have come from American English? Guess, then read the answer to this question.

blizzard, blurb, cafeteria, cocktail (the drink), *electrocute, jazz, radio, stooge, belittle, swamp, snazzy, kissogram, trial* (as a verb), *unsackable, truish*

Why did American English develop such different characteristics from British English? The first permanent English settlement in America was at Jamestown in Virginia in 1607. The settlers came mainly from the eastern and southern counties of Britain (a few from the Midlands). The 'Pilgrim Fathers' and the *Mayflower* landed at Cape Cod in 1620, and made a settlement at Plymouth, Massachusetts. These settlers were mainly from south-west England. Most might be described as economic, religious (especially, Puritan) and/or political refugees. By 1640, some estimate that there were approximately 25,000 immigrants. From the eighteenth century onwards, there was massive immigration from Ireland and Scotland. These immigrants settled along the eastern coast, especially around Philadelphia, but also played a large part as frontier people, opening up the west. There was also, of course, settlement by speakers of many other languages: Spanish, French, Dutch, German, African, etc. Note that from the beginning, then, American English had its own dialectal mix, and thus was likely to develop in different directions from British English. Moreover, with the loss of regular contact with British English speakers, and brought into contact with a new environment and native Indian languages, it is not surprising that American English acquired its own characteristics.

EXERCISE

11.3 The influence of the environment and native Indian languages on the development of English in North America is most obvious in vocabulary. Go through list (a) below and make sure you know what aspects of the environment are being referred to (consult an etymological dictionary, if in doubt); then go through list (b) and investigate the etymology of these words.

    (a) *back country, bluff, garter-snake, groundhog, notch (as a landscape feature), prairie*

    (b) *canoe, chipmunk, moose, racoon, toboggan, tapioca*

It is sometimes said that American English has features that are archaic from the point of view of British English. Let's take some features of General American English (hereafter GA) – what is sometimes described as the 'standard' American dialect and accent, typically found in the middle states and in the west – and compare them with British RP and standard written English.

- In GA the vowel in words such as *ask, dance, bath* and *half* is [æ], not [ɑː] as in RP. The [æ] began to be lost in southern British English from the late eighteenth century.

- In GA the letter <r> is pronounced in all positions, but in RP it is only pronounced before vowels (e.g. *very, paragraph*). It is claimed that post-vocalic <r> began to disappear from London speech from the late seventeenth century.

- In RP the vowels in pairs like *cot/caught* are distinct: [ɒ] and [ɔː] respectively. However, in GA these vowels have merged in various ways. For example, often in GA [ɑ] is used in both *cot* and *caught*. This is similar to an older pronunciation in British English: note that Chaucer spelt 'not' as *nat*.

- Perhaps the most striking morphological difference between GA and British English is the use of the past participle form *gotten* in GA. This was in fact the usual form in British English two centuries ago. [Check Text 6(b) for an example.]

- In GA the season following summer is referred to as the *fall*, as used to be the case in British English where the term *autumn* is now used.

- In GA the word *mad* is frequently used to mean 'angry', a sense that was fairly common in British EMod.E, but is less so now.

EXERCISE

11.4 How valid are the comparisons made in the above paragraph for *all* of American English and *all* of British English? If you are familiar with British English, consider whether any of the supposedly American features do in fact appear in British English. If you are familiar with American English, consider whether any of the supposedly British features do in fact appear in American English.

There never have been any major linguistic differences between British and American English. Moreover, the last hundred years or so have seen increasing similarity between British and American English. This has partly been due to ever-improving communication systems, but also to the impact of American culture, notably through television and film.

EXERCISE

11.5 Test your familiarity with near-equivalent words in British and American English by filling the gaps.

British English	American English	American English	British English
trainers		candy	
vest		carryall	
waistcoat		cookie	
motorway		cot	
torch		diaper	
braces		drapes	
petrol		faucet	
shop assistant		public school	

Other important varieties of English include those of Australia, Canada, Ireland, New Zealand and South Africa, where English is principally a native language, and also various countries in Africa, the subcontinent of India, the Caribbean and south-east Asia, where English is principally a second language. Moreover, they have developed through different kinds of event. Dick Leith identifies three different kinds. In countries like America and Australia, the indigenous population was displaced; in many countries in Africa (e.g. Nigeria) and the subcontinent of India, a tiny English minority controlled the indigenous population, allowing a select elite access to education and the learning of English; and finally in the Caribbean (and some south-east Asian countries) the indigenous population is replaced with labour from elsewhere (e.g. West Africa in the case of the Caribbean). It is the final kind of event that can lead to particularly interesting developments, notably the development of PIDGINS and CREOLES.

Pidgins
Creoles

The history of Jamaican English is the history of a pidgin and a creole (and perhaps something beyond that). A key feature of a pidgin is that it has no native speakers. It comes about when people need to communicate, but have no language in common. Such was the situation when slaves speaking many different languages were gathered on the west coast of Africa and then transported to the Americas and the Caribbean. Features of a pidgin are that it is *regularised*, *mixed* and *reduced*. The grammar is regularised, so that redundancies are lost. For example, there is no need to say *ten bottles*, with an -s plural marker when we know from the number that it is plural; and there is no need to add the <s> marking the third person present singular in a sentence like *He talks to me*, when the pronoun *he* makes it clear that it is the third person singular and the fact that it is present is easily retrievable from the context. Mixing means that elements are drawn from different input languages. For example, though the bulk of vocabulary is sourced from English, a number of African words, such as *nyam* (= 'to eat'), are mixed in. It is reduced in the sense that it serves a limited set of functions (e.g. just to facilitate trading). A creole, in contrast, might be described as a second generation pidgin: it is learnt as a native language. Like a pidgin, a creole is still relatively regularised and mixed compared with the original input languages, but it is no longer reduced. It develops a range of styles, used for a range of purposes, including, for example, a written literature (the 1992 Nobel Prize for Literature was awarded to the Caribbean poet Derek Walcott). This increase in function goes hand in hand with an increase in vocabulary and grammatical complexity. But note what is happening if this process continues: the creole is moving in the opposite direction to how it came **Decreolisation** about in the first place: it undergoes DECREOLISATION.

EXERCISE

11.6 Guess the background of the speaker of Text 8(c), including where they come from. Draw up a list of features that strike you as distinctive. Now read the answer to this exercise.

Earlier in this book, we noted the settlement of Britain by the Anglo-Saxons, Scandinavians and French, and the linguistic consequences of bringing different languages into contact. Some commentators have argued that English experienced a kind of creolisation during ME. English too has undergone grammatical regularisation and lexical mixing. Whether this really amounts to creolisation partly depends on how one defines the labels, but it seems unlikely for various reasons. For example, Old Norse and Old Danish, as mentioned earlier, were partly intelligible to the Anglo-Saxon English speaker, so there was little communicative need for a pidgin; it is the French colonial conquerors who typically became bilingual and eventually shifted to English, not the other way round, as is typical of pidgins and creoles; and, importantly, the regularisation of English grammar pre-dates Scandinavian or French influence: evidence of regularisation appears, for instance, in the Lindisfarne Gospels, which pre-date Scandinavian and French settlement/invasion.

Though such dramatic settlements have not been repeated in Britain, immigration is still an important factor in explaining the development of many varieties of English. For example, features of Irish English, such as the use of *yous* for plural *you*, can be heard in Liverpool. Indeed, this particular feature of Irish English can also be heard in Australia and many parts of the United States. All these places have experienced Irish immigration in the last 200 years.

EXERCISES

11.7 Listen to the recordings for London and Bradford (Yorkshire, N. England) at: http://www.phon.ox.ac.uk/~esther/ivyweb/. You are in fact listening to specific varieties that combine features of the regional English accent/dialect with features of the original language of a relatively recent immigrant population. The London speakers are of Caribbean descent; the Bradford speakers are bilingual Punjabi-English speakers.

11.8 The words below are now fairly well known in most world Englishes. But in which variety of English did each of the words originate? Where possible, also try to identify which language supplied the word to English.

aardvark, amok, apartheid, bangle, boomerang, bungalow, calypso, caribou, commando, cot, dungaree, guru, jodhpurs, juggernaut, jungle, kangaroo, kayak, kiwi, loot, parka, punch (the drink), pundit, pyjama, reggae, safari, shampoo, thug, veranda, voodoo, yoga, zebra

DISCUSSION POINT

It is sometimes claimed that English as an international language will 'succumb' to the same fate as Latin. Around 2,000 years ago, Latin was used throughout Western Europe, North Africa and Asia Minor (i.e. including the area covered by today's Turkey). Today, Latin is a dead language, and its descendants – such as Italian, French and Spanish – are separate languages. Do you think this prophecy is likely to be fulfilled? Will English become a group of English languages that are not mutually comprehensible? If you are part of a group, set up a debate: half argue in support of the prophecy, and half against it. (*Hint:* It may help to consider spoken and written forms of language separately.)

SUMMARY

- The last few centuries have seen the rapid expansion of English in terms of where it is found in the world, the number of uses to which it is put and the number of users.
- The most important national varieties are British English and American English, owing to imperial and economic power.
- In the beginning – the early seventeenth century – American English and British English grew apart, but more recently, with improved communications and the popularity of American culture, they are growing closer together.
- American English does contain a few features that are archaic from the point of view of British English. However, how many archaic features can be identified rather depends on which particular varieties of British and American English are considered.
- Distinctive varieties of English have developed across the globe, each in their own unique way. Some Englishes have developed through creolisation.
- Immigration is still an important factor in the development of many varieties of English.

FOLLOW-UP READING

David Crystal covers world Englishes in some detail in his *Encyclopedia of the English Language* (Cambridge: Cambridge University Press, 2003). On pp. 92–105 he describes the establishment of varieties of English outside Britain; on pp. 106–15 he discusses English as a 'world language' and considers the future of English; and on pp. 306–17 he focuses on American English, and on pp. 328–57 other varieties of English. Pages 358–63 contain an interesting discussion of aspects of global English. A relevant and easy-to-read commentary can also be found in R. McCrum, W. Cran and R. MacNeil's *The Story of English* (London: Faber & Faber/BBC, 1992), chapters 6–9. If you are interested in how varieties of language develop as a result of contact between languages, try Mark Sebba's *Contact Languages: Pidgins and Creoles* (London: Macmillan, 1997), where chapters 7 and 9 consider varieties touched on in Exercises 11.6 and 11.7. An excellent and accessible assessment of whether ME can be said to have experienced creolisation is Barbara Fennell's *A History of English: A Sociolinguistic Approach* (Oxford: Blackwell, pp. 125–31). This book also has useful chapters on North American English and world Englishes generally.

APPENDIX I

Reading an OED Entry

Below is the first part of the *OED* entry for the word *experience*. Note that guidance on abbreviations can be found at the beginning of the dictionary.

Square brackets enclose etymological information. Reconstructed, the text reads: 'adopted from **Fr**ench *expérience*, which was **ad**apted from **L**atin *experientia*, which was **f**ormed from *experientem*, the **pr**esent **participle** of *experiri*, meaning to try, put to the test' (abbreviations are in bold print). The terms 'adopted' and 'adapted' both mean that a word has been borrowed from another language, but 'adapted' also signals that the word has been altered in some way.

Pronunciation information. The apostrophe indicates that the following syllable is stressed.

Grammatical information, i.e. *n.* = a noun.

The dagger indicates that sense 1. a. is now obsolete.

First citation date: the earliest recorded occurrence of the word *experience*.

The period during which the following spelling variants are found. 4–6 = fourteenth to sixteenth centuries.

The author, followed by the work and then the quotation.

experience (ɛkˈspɪərɪəns), n. Also 4–6 experiens, –jans, –yens, 5–6 experyence. [a. Fr. *expérience*, ad. L. *experientia*, f. *experient–em*, pr. pple. of *experīrī* to try, put to the test.]

† **1. a.** The action of putting to the test; trial. *to make experience of*: to make trial of. *Obs.*

1388 WYCLIF *Gen.* xlii. 15 Now y schal take experience [1382 experyment] of ȝou.

1393 GOWER *Conf.* I. 14 At Avynon thexperience Therof haþ ȝoue an euidence.

1596 SPENSER *F. Q.* v. i. 7 Of all the which . . She [Astræa] caused him [Artegall] to make experience Vpon wild beasts.

APPENDIX II

The Indo-European family tree

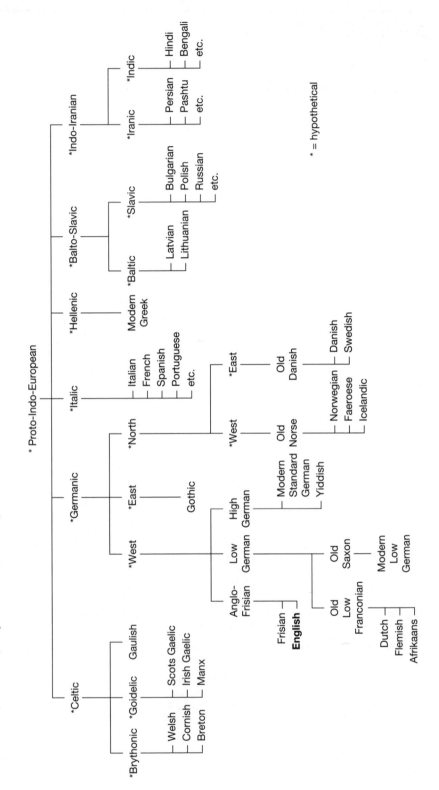

APPENDIX III

Phonetic transcription

The set of symbols used to represent speech sounds in this book is based on that used by David Crystal in his *Encyclopedia of the English Language* (Cambridge: Cambridge University Press, 2003, pp. 237–45), which in turn is based on that of the British phonetician A.C. Gimson in *An Introduction to the Pronunciation of English* (1st edn, London: Edward Arnold, 1962). Readers from the United States may wish to note that Crystal (p. 237) shows how Gimson's system relates to that used in Fromkin and Rodman's *An Introduction to Language* (5th edn, New York: Holt, Rinehart & Winston, 1992), a widely used textbook in the United States (also, in Appendix VI, I give a web link illustrating differences between English and American vowel sounds).

Different speakers may pronounce words differently, so it is difficult to suggest a word that illustrates a particular speech sound for everybody. In common with the books noted above, I use Received Pronunciation (RP), a well-known British accent (sometimes referred to as the Queen's English or BBC English). (We look at the development of RP in Unit 10.) Beneath the symbols given on p. 106, I have suggested a few of the variations speakers of other accents might have (and you can hear many of these by following the relevant web links in Appendix VI). Some of these variations are considered in Unit 9. The illustrative words I use are almost all taken from Crystal (pp. 237 and 242). Note that, on the web, you can click on a phonetic symbol and hear it (explore the web links in Appendix VI!).

The symbols below are divided into consonants and vowels. The colon is used to signal a long vowel. The convention in this book for indicating a speech sound symbol, as opposed to spelling, is to place the symbol between square brackets, e.g. [v] for the last sound in *of*.

Consonants

p	*pie, up*	f	*fee, off*
b	*by, ebb*	v	*view, of*
t	*tie, at*	θ	*thigh, oath*
d	*die, odd*	ð	*they, booth*
k	*coo, ache*	s	*so, us*
g	*go, egg*	z	*zoo, ooze*
tʃ	*chew, each*	ʃ	*shoe, ash*
dʒ	*jaw, edge*	ʒ	*genre, rouge*

h	*he*
m	*me, am*
n	*no, in*
ŋ	*hang*
l	*lie, eel*
r	*row, ear (not RP)*
w	*way*
j	*you*

Glottal stop

Variations: Instead of [t], many speakers, stereotypically Cockney and urban speakers, will use a GLOTTAL STOP [ʔ]. For example, in words like *bottle* the sound represented by <t> is replaced by one that is made by closing the vocal cords and does not involve the tip of the tongue. Writers sometimes suggest glottal stops with apostrophes (e.g. *be'er* for *better*). In the United States, speakers often replace [t] between vowels (e.g. in words like *butter*) with a sound which is closer to [d].

Vowels

iː	*sea, feet, me, field*	ɜː	*bird, her, turn, learn*
ɪ	*him, big, village, women*	ə	*the, oppose, sofa, about*
ɛ	*get, fetch, head, Thames*	eɪ	*ape, waist, they, say*
æ	*sat, hand, ban, plait*	aɪ	*time, cry, die, high*
ʌ	*sun, son, blood, does*	ɔɪ	*boy, toy, noise, voice*
ɑː	*calm, are, father, car*	əʊ	*so, road, toe, know*
ɒ	*dog, lock, swan, cough*	ɒʊ	*out, how, house, found*
ɔː	*all, saw, cord, more*	ɪə	*deer, here, fierce, near*
ʊ	*put, wolf, good, look*	eə	*care, air, bare, bear*
uː	*soon, do, soup, shoe*	ʊə	*poor, sure, tour, lure*

Variations: Speakers in the north of England do not have the vowel [ʌ], but instead use [ʊ]. Scottish and Irish accents do not have long [ɑː], but may use a short [a] or a vowel towards [æ]. For many speakers of American English, the vowels [ɒ] and [ɔː] may not be distinguished (many speakers are likely to use [ɑ] for both). For speakers who pronounce <r> when it follows a vowel, the vowels that precede <r> are likely to be shorter. For example, the RP pronunciations of *car, bird, deer, care* and *poor* are [kɑː], [bɜːd], [dɪə], [keə] and [pʊə], but for many speakers from the United States they may be closer to [kɑr], [bərd], [dɪr], [ker] and [pʊr].

APPENDIX IV

A 'mini-corpus' of texts

TEXT 1

This text comes from the prologue of the *Anglo-Saxon Chronicle* (specifically, the version known as the *Peterborough Chronicle*), a yearly history of important events, written in the ninth century. A word-for-word translation is given in the line below. The original text appears in the 'insular' style of handwriting, so-called to distinguish the Anglo-Saxon style from those on the continent. Don't panic – it's not as incomprehensible as it looks! You will come across 'wynn', a character from the old Runic alphabet, which was written <ƿ> (looking somewhat like a modern <p>). This character was not familiar to Norman scribes, who replaced it in the eleventh century by <w>. You will see the character 'yogh' <ȝ>, which gave rise to today's <g>. Today, it would typically be replaced by <g>, <y> or <gh>. Today's <r> had a longer downstroke – thus <ɼ> – but is otherwise similar. The character 'thorn' <ð>, another Runic symbol, was roughly equivalent to today's <th> (it was often written without the cross-bar, i.e. <þ>). Our <s> was written in various ways, including <ſ> (so-called 'long s'), <ʃ> and <s> (the symbol with which we are familiar). You will find that our <sh> is rendered <ſc> (modern <sc>). The symbol <⁊> is roughly equivalent to today's ampersand symbol <&>. Below, the text in italics is a word-for-word translation; the text immediately above renders the original in modern characters (brackets indicate either that a completely different character is used or that there is no simple correspondence between the characters).

Bƿittene iȝland iſ ehta hund mila lanȝ
Brittene i(g)land is ehta hund mila lang
Britain island is eight hundred miles long

⁊ τρα hunð bραð . ⁊ heρ ρınð on þıs
& t(w)a hund brad & her sind on (th)is
& two hundred broad & here are on this

ıȝlanðe fıf ȝeþeoðe . enȝlıſc . ⁊ bρıτ
i(g)lande fif (g)e(th)eode englisc & brit
island five languages English & Brit-

τıſc . ⁊ pılſc . ⁊ ſcÿττıſc . ⁊ pÿhτıſc. ⁊
tisc & (w)ilsc & scyttisc & pyhtisc &
tish & Welsh & Scottish & Pictish &

bocleðen . Eρeſτ peρon buȝenð þıſeſ
bocleden Erest (w)eron bu(g)end (th)ises
book-Latin first were inhabitants of this

lanðeſ bρıττeſ .
landes brittes
land Britons

TEXT 2

This text is from John of Trevisa's translation of the *Polychronicon*, a history of the world written in Latin by Ralph Higden. (An image of this manuscript can be seen at http://special.lib.gla.ac.uk/exhibns/Chaucer/contemporaries.html, along with other important ME texts.) The translation was finished in 1387, and represents the southern dialect, or, more specifically, that of Gloucestershire. Here Trevisa writes about the accents of England. (There are several existing manuscripts of the *Polychronicon*. The text here is O.F. Emerson's transcription of the British Library's Cotton Tiberiius D VII manuscript. The punctuation is not original, and Emerson appears to have modernised the usage of the letters <v> and <u>.)

[. . .] for men of þe est wiþ men of þe west, as hyt [= *it*] were undur þe same party of hevene, acordeþ more in sounyng of speche [i.e. in pronunciation] þan men of þe norþ wiþ men of þe souþ. þerfore hyt ys þat Mercii [= *the Mercians*], þat buþ [= *are*] men of myddel Engelond, as hyt were parteners of þe endes, understondeþ betre þe syde longages, norþeron and souþeron, þan norþeron and souþeron understondeþ eyþer oþer. Al þe longage of þe Norþhumbres, and specialych at ȝork, ys so scharp, slyttyng [= *cutting*] and frotyng [= *grating*] and unschape, þat we souþeron men may þat longage vnneþe [= *hardly*] vnderstonde. Y trowe [= *believe*] þat þat ys bycause þat a [= *they*] buþ ny3 [= *near*] to strange men and aliens [= *foreigners*] þat spekeþ strangelych, and also bycause þat þe kynges of Engelond woneþ [= *dwell*] alwey fer fram þat contray; for a buþ more yturned [= *turned*] to þe souþ contray, and 3ef [= *if*] a goþ to þe norþ contray a goþ wiþ gret help and strengthe.

TEXT 3

This text is part of William Caxton's prologue to the *Eneydos* (his translation of the French version of the Latin poem *The Aeneid* by Virgil), printed in 1490. He recounts a story about some merchants who tried to ask for eggs in Kent.

> And certaynly our langage now vsed varyeth ferre from that. whiche was vsed and spoken whan I was borne / For we englysshe men / ben borne vnder the domynacyon of the mone. whiche is neuer stedfaste / but euer wauerynge / wexynge one season / and waneth & dyscreaseth another season / And that comyn englysshe that is spoken in one shyre varyeth from a nother. In so moche that in my dayes happened that certayn marchauntes were in a shippe in tamyse [= *the river Thames*] for to haue sayled ouer the see into 3elande [= *Holland*] / and for lacke of wynde thei taryed atte forlond [= *Foreland*]. and wente to lande for to refreshe them And one of theym named sheffelde a mercer cam in to an hows and axed for mete. and specyally he axyd after eggys And the good wyf answerde. that she coude speke no frenshe. And the marchaunt was angry. for he also coude speke no frenshe. but wold haue hadde egges / and she vnderstode hym not / And thenne at laste a nother sayd that he wolde haue eyren / then the good wyf sayd that she vnderstod hym wel / Loo what sholde a man in thyse dayes now wryte. egges or eyren / certaynly it is harde to playse euery man / by cause of dyuersite & chaunge of langage.

TEXT 4

This text is a letter written in 1497. The Celys were London merchants. Here Richard Cely writes 'in haste' to his family to tell them of a battle between France and Burgundy.

> I grete you wyll I late [= *let*] you wit [= *know*] of seche tydyng as I here Thomas blehom hatth a letter from caleys [= *Calais*] the weche ys of a batell done on sater^{day} last paste be syde trywyn [= *Tirwin*] be [= *by*]

the dwke of borgan & the frynche kyng the weche batell be gane on
sater day at iiij [= 4] of the cloke at after non and laste tyll nyght &
meche blode schede of bothe pertys and the dwke of borgan hathe the
fylde and the worschepe the dwke of borgan hathe gette meche
ordenons [= *ordnance*] of frenche kyngys and hathe slayne v or vj ml
[= *5 or 6 thousand*] frensche men wryte on thorys day noe in haste

p Rc cely [= *(per) by Richard Cely*]

TEXT 5

The following passage is from the *Merrie Tales of Skelton* (1567). In this
tale, Skelton, a parson, tries to persuade a cobbler to go to war. Copy
editing errors occur relatively often in this period, as exemplified by *thig*
(=thing). The use of the tilde in <õ> and <ã> indicates the omission of
a following <n>.

Neybour, you be a tall
man, and in the Kynges warres
you must bere a standard. A
standerd, said the cobler, what a thig
is that. Skeltõ saide: it is a great
banner, such a one as thou dooest
vse to beare in Rogacyon weeke,
and a Lordes, or a Knyghtes, or
a gentle mannes armes shall bee
vpon it, and the Souldiers that
be vnder the afore sayde persons
fayghtynge vnder thy Banner:
fayghtynge, sayde the Cobbeler:
I can no skil in faighting: no said
Skelton, thou shalte not fayght,
but holde vp, and aduaunce the
bãner. By my fay, sayd the cobler,
I can no skill in the matter. Well
sayd Skeltõ there is no reamedie
but thou shalte forthe to dooe the
Kynges seruice in hys Warres,
for in all this Countrey theare is
not a more likelier manne to dooe
suche as feate as thou arte. Syr
sayde the Cobbeler: I wyll
geue you a fatte Capon, that I
maye bee at home. No, sayde
Skelton, I wyll not haue none
of thy Capons: for thou shalte
doe the Kyng seruice in his wars.

TEXT 6

These extracts are from the Authorised Version of the Bible, which was
published in 1611. Extract (a) is from the New Testament, Luke 6:
27–32; extract (b) is from the Old Testament, Ezekiel 28: 1–4.

(a)

But I say vnto you which heare, Loue your enemies, doe good to them
which hate you,

Bless them that curse you, & pray for them which despitefully vse you.

And vnto him that smiteth thee on the *one* cheeke, offer also the other: and him that taketh away thy cloake, forbid not to take thy coat also.

Give to euery man that asketh of thee, and of him that taketh away thy goods, aske them not againe.

And as yee would that men should doe to you, doe yee also to them likewise.

For if yee loue them which loue you, what thanke haue ye? for sinners also loue those that loue them.

(b)
THe word of the LORD came againe vnto me, saying,

Sonne of man, say vnto the prince of Tyrus.

Thus saith the Lord GOD; Because thine heart is lifted vp, and thou hast said, I *am* a God, I sit *in* the seate of God, in the middest of the seas; yet thou *art* a man, and not God, though thou set thine heart as the heart of God.

Behold, thou *art* wiser than Daniel: there is no secret that they can hide from thee.

With thy wisdome and with thine vnderstanding thou hast gotten thee riches, and hast gotten gold and siluer into thy treasures.

TEXT 7

This text is from John Milton's *Areopagitica*, published in 1644.

I deny not, but that it is of greatest concernment in the Church and Commonwealth, to have a vigilant eye how Bookes demeane themselves as well as men; and thereafter to confine, imprison, and do sharpest justice on them as malefactors: For Books are not absolutely dead things, but doe contain a potencie of life in them to be as active as that soule was whose progeny they are; nay they do preserve as in a violl the purest efficacie and extraction of that living intellect that bred them. I know they are as lively, and as vigorously productive, as those fabulous Dragons teeth; and being sown up and down, may chance to spring up armed men. And yet on the other hand unlesse warinesse be us'd, as good almost kill a Man as kill a good Book; who kills a Man kills a reasonable creature, Gods Image; but hee who destroyes a good Booke, kills reason it selfe, kills the Image of God, as it were in the eye.

TEXT 8

These texts represent different varieties of today's English. Text (a) is an insurance condition that appears on the back of Comet Superstore receipts. It is supposedly legally binding. Text (b) is the first part of a text that accompanies an advertisement for a child's drink. Information about the speaker of (c) is given in the answer to Exercise 11.6. The spelling of this text has been altered to convey something of the pronunciation. The symbol % represents a glottal stop. $ represents an <l> pronounced more like [w].

(a)
All of the express terms, conditions and exceptions applicable to the insurance of the product are set out in the Certificate. The scope and extent of the insurance cannot be extended without the express written authority of the Insurer.

(b)
Who understands I need almost as much iron as Daddy?
   It may surprise you to learn that from the age of 6 months, a baby needs 90% as much iron as a 30 year old man. However, cow's milk is too low in iron and vitamins A & D to be a main drink for a growing baby.

(c)
One day me met a witch [. . .] me saw her dere, me sit down an she tell me all the story alrigh%? One story was about the ghost she see – this is the story whe she tell me wha% she see, alright. She, one day she te$ me dat she saw a ghost – or somefing like a ghost, a person who come in the house – she te$ me she pick up a brick and break i bones – de ting run like she no know what.

APPENDIX V

Some answers

UNIT 1   THE BIRTH OF ENGLISH

1.1 Placenames with a Celtic link tend to survive in areas that did not see settlement by other peoples, notably the Germanic tribes – the 'Anglo-Saxons'. Thus, such placenames dominate areas of Scotland to the north of Edinburgh and areas in the west of Britain, particularly Ireland, Wales and Cornwall.

1.3 (a) You probably found that surprisingly few placenames are transferred British placenames. Many placenames that look like transferred British placenames turn out to be biographic – the names of British aristocrats, for example. Aboriginal placenames make up a substantial proportion of Australian placenames. (This proportion does not in fact reflect the rather small impact of Aboriginal languages on Australian English.)

    (b) You probably discovered that British influence was highest for eastern states, French for southern states and Spanish for the western states. This, of course, reflects the spheres of influence of those three colonial powers.

UNIT 2   INVESTIGATING CHANGE IN ENGLISH

2.1 *Writing*: Unfamiliar letters include <þ> (later replaced by <th>, as in *this*) and 7 (which is similar to our ampersand symbol *&*). Many words have different spellings from today. Clearly, our <sh> used to be written <sc> (e.g. *englisc, brittisc, wilsc*). The main punctuation mark here is the 'punctus' <·>, which we would think of as a full-stop; note, however, that it is positioned in the middle of the line and that it appears where we would not expect it. Capitals are rarely used and are notably absent from proper nouns (e.g. *englisc*, *brittisc, wilsc*).

Structure: Note that there were many other ways in which one could make a plural noun apart from adding an <s>. Look at the equivalent words for 'miles', 'languages' and 'inhabitants': they are all plurals, but none is marked with an <s>. In translating OE one often has to supply extra prepositions, such as *of*. The order of words in the last 'sentence' is strange from today's point of view, particularly with regard to the position of the verb 'were'.

Words: Some words are not used today (e.g. *geþeode, bugend*). There is even a different word for 'are'.

Meaning: The words *brittisc* and *brittes* do not have today's meaning. They refer to the Celtic-speaking tribes that used to inhabit Britain. In fact, *brittisc* and *wilsc* were one and the same language – Brito-Welsh – and this explains why the writer says that there are five languages and then appears to list six.

2.2 Various factors influence people's perceptions of what is new. One factor relates to the fact that change occurs faster and more dramatically at some linguistic levels than others. Typically, change at the levels of phonology (sound) and grammar (structure) takes place rather slowly (and, for beginners, is more difficult to describe), compared with change at the level of lexis (words), which can be much faster. So, it is likely that most of your examples are lexical ones.

2.3 In normal fluent speech, many sounds apparently represented by the letters of spelling are not actually said, regardless of the social status of the speaker. It is very often the case that word-final sounds like [t] and [d] ('alveolar-dentals') are not pronounced in connected speech.

2.4 Typically, the older pronunciation stresses the first syllable, and the newer pronunciation the second syllable. This development has not been followed in the United States, where the first syllable is stressed.

UNIT 3 SPELLINGS AND SPEECH SOUNDS

3.1 Some observations might be: (1) <c> can be [k] as in *cat*, or [s] as in *centre*, (2) <a> can represent a range of sounds, including [æ] as in *cat*, [e] as in many, [ə] as in *again*, and [eɪ] as in *case*, and (3) <t> is indeed often [t], though a frequent case where it is not is when it is followed by an <h>.

3.3 These, of course, are some of the now infamous silent consonants of English spelling. Medial <w> and <l>, and initial <w>, <g> and <k> were almost certainly once pronounced. The conditions for these changes seem to be as follows (if you are not sure about some of the terms used below, e.g. 'low vowel', read this again after you have completed Unit 3):

sword → when [w] is after [s] and before certain vowels (e.g. the vowel of *switch* is excluded)
walk, half, folk → when [l] is after a low vowel and before a consonant (e.g. *milk and fall* are excluded)
wreck, write, wring → when [w] is before [r] and word-initial
gnat, gnarl, gnaw → when [g] is before [n] and word-initial
knee, know, knight → when [k] is before [n] and word-initial

3.4 You should be able to hear [x]. This would seem to fit the kind of lenition we were discussing in the commentary; in other words, [k] → [x] → [h] → [ø] (the final symbol indicates zero). The latest research suggests that this feature is increasing in the Liverpool accent, but it is limited to that accent. One might speculate whether one day most English speakers will follow this change.

3.5 The letter <v> is used at the beginning of a word and <u> medially, where today we would use either <v> or <u>. This is the general pattern used by many other writers. In Texts 3 and 4, <i> and <y> do seem fairly interchangeable. We would need to consider a larger sample of texts to come to any firm conclusions.

3.6 You might want to consider words such as *ghost* and *ghoul*, and *graffiti* and *anti*.

3.7 (a) The addition of the final *-e* (after a single consonant) signals a preceding long vowel. A few counter-examples, such as *some* and *give*, can be found.

(b) The doubled consonant signals a preceding short vowel. Counter-examples, such as *fall*, are rare.

3.8 (a) Potential problems include silent letters and the fact that schwa [ə] has no corresponding letter, but can be represented in a number of different ways in English.

(b) These words have troublesome spellings because they have been borrowed from other languages – Latin, French and Greek – and reflect the spelling conventions of those languages.

UNIT 4   BORROWING WORDS

4.2   (a) The large proportion of French-derived vocabulary in Text 8(a) contributes to its legal stylistic flavour. The vocabulary of Text 8(b) is overwhelmingly Germanic, making it a very accessible text with a conversational flavour – something that is clearly in the advertiser's interests. There are just three exceptions: *surprise* (a fifteenth-century loan from Old French), *vitamins* (a twentieth-century loan from Latin) and % (= *per cent*) (a sixteenth-century loan from Latin, probably via Italian).

(b) Text 4 contains largely Germanic vocabulary, except for some words derived from French. Text 7 also includes a number of words borrowed from Latin. This can be partly explained by noting that Text 4 was written before the dramatic Renaissance influx of Latin vocabulary. It also reflects the fact that Milton in Text 7 was writing a scholarly text for a highly educated audience.

4.4   Keith Waterhouse's advice seems to be of little value. Think of contexts where you would use one of a pair and then try swapping it with the other. You'll find a number of differences. Taking the pair *penniless* and *penurious* as an example, you'll find: *penniless* is only used to describe humans, whereas *penurious* never is; *penurious* has a slightly more negative tinge to its meaning than *penniless*, which tends simply to describe a state; *penurious* only ever occurs before the noun to which it refers, whereas *penniless* can occur both before or after; and *penurious* is a more formal word than *penniless*.

UNIT 5   NEW WORDS FROM OLD

5.1   *anti-dis-establish-ment-arian-ism*.

5.7   *snail mail* (open compound, contrasting with speedy *e-mail*), *road rage* (open compound, modelled on *roid rage*, which is a clipped form of *steroid rage*, referring to bursts of violent behaviour that that drug can cause), *way* (functional conversion of a noun to adverb, or, more precisely, intensifier, like *very*, probably, an American English innovation), *detox* (a clip of detoxification; not that new – the OED records it in 1970), *fantabulous* (blend of *fantastic* and *fabulous*, but this is much older than one might think – the OED records it in 1959), and *IMHO* (acronym for 'in my humble opinion', used frequently on the internet and in text messaging; may be gaining more general currency).

UNIT 6 CHANGING MEANINGS

6.1 *Woman* suggests physical aspects; *lady* suggests social aspects.

6.2 Examples (b), (c), (e), (g) and (h) contain metaphors.

UNIT 7 GRAMMAR I: NOUNS

7.1 Introspection is extremely unreliable here. Most people think that the 'foreign' etymological plural is the 'correct' one, and so usually try to supply it, even though they might not actually use it. Interestingly, when asked about *octopus*, they usually recognise it as a foreign *-us* ending requiring a plural *-i* marking, giving *octopi*. The plural *-i* ending for words ending singular *-us* was one of a number of ways in which the plural was marked in Latin. Unfortunately, *octopus* is borrowed from Greek, and so the etymological plural is *octopodes*.

7.2 (a)
  (1) He (subject) sees him (object)
  (2) Him (object) he (subject) sees
  (3) He (subject) sees his (possessor) face

  (b) In Text 6, the usage of second-person pronouns seems to be grammatical (e.g. *ye* is only used as a plural subjective form, *you* as a plural objective form), even though this was not generally the case at the time. But note that we are looking at biblical language, which by its very nature is archaic. In contrast, the usage of second-person pronouns in Text 5 is governed by social and pragmatic factors, not grammatical. Both you and thou-forms are used, even though there is never more than one addressee. One might predict, on the basis of social factors, that the Parson would use thou-forms to the cobbler and the cobbler you-forms to the Parson. The cobbler does indeed use 'you' to the Parson: 'Syr sayde the Cobbeler: I wyll geue you a fatte Capon'. Note that he also uses 'sir'. The use of 'you' fits his generally polite and deferential stance. But the Parson also uses 'you': 'Neybour, you be a tall man, and in the Kynges warres you must bere a standard'. This is not what the social theory would predict. But remember that this is where the Parson is attempting pragmatically to 'butter up' the cobbler, and thereby persuade him to go to war. Thus, he not only uses 'Neybour', but also uses 'you', and thereby politely implies that they are on an equal footing. Thereafter, the Parson switches to thou-forms. Three of such usages co-occur with 'shalte'. The word 'shall' at this time expressed obligation: the Parson is exerting his authority in saying the cobbler is obliged to go to war. The use of thou-forms could reinforce this strategy by emphasising the cobbler's subordinate status.

UNIT 8   GRAMMAR II: VERBS

8.1 • *I walk the dog*: no inflection = the base form.
   • *She walks the dog*: base form + *s* = the third person singular.
   • *She walked the dog*: base form + *ed* = the simple past. However, for many verbs the +*ed* inflection is also used to form the *past participle*. What is the past participle? Typically, the past participle follows the verbs *have* or *be*, as in (1) *Helen has walked the dog* or (2) *The dog was walked by Helen*. Note that for some verbs the simple past and the past participle can have different forms, e.g. *She rode into town* vs. *She has ridden into town*.
   • *She is walking the dog*: base form + *ing* = the present participle. In this example, the present participle signals that the action has not been completed, but is ongoing. Compare with *Helen has walked the dog* above, where the action has been completed. Both examples are present tense, as expressed by *is* and *has*, but the present participle of the first signals that the action is ongoing, whereas the past participle of the second signals that it has been completed. The first is present *progressive*, the second present *perfect*. Progressive and perfect express different *aspect*.

8.2 The *-eth* inflection was archaic at this time. This explains why *-s* does not appear in Text 6: biblical language tends to be archaic. It is worth mentioning here that EMod.E poets, including Shakespeare, exploited the fact that *-eth* provided a word with an extra syllable (compare *heareth* and *hears*). This could help with the construction of the metre.

8.3 Some examples: drunken sailor, grief stricken, molten lead, shrunken head.

8.5 Can they stand alone? Yes, there are examples of both alone in Text 5 (e.g. *I can no skill, thou shalte forthe*). Do they carry inflections? Note *thou shalte*, which carries the second person inflection. *Shalt*, as well as *wilt*, survived well into EModE. Has the meaning changed? The instances of *thou shalte* express obligation, but note that a more familiar predictive meaning was current: *a gentle* *mannes arms shall bee upon it.* Both instances of *I can no skil* have the older meaning 'know'.

UNIT 9   DIALECTS IN BRITISH ENGLISH

9.4 If you are using the *OED*, the odd one out for *sword* is *zuord*, and for *father* the ones beginning with initial <v>, e.g. *vader*. The key difference between [s] and [z], and [f] and [v] is the 'voicing' of the second items in the pairs. Voicing involves the vibration of the vocal folds in the larynx. Put your fingers in your ears and practise saying the above pairs (you should hear the buzzing more clearly). Using the voiced variants, i.e. [z] and [v], is today the stereotypical feature of south-western accents, though in reality these features are less used now. In the *OED vader* is marked out as a southern dialect feature. The southern dialect area used to include Kent, which is why *zuord* occurs in a Kentish text, *The Ayenbite of Inwit* ('Remorse of conscience') (a translation by Dan Michel of St Augustine's Abbey, Canterbury, Kent, finished in 1340).

9.5 (a) The pronunciation [uː] can still be heard in Northumberland and Scotland.

(b) As is stated in Unit 3, speakers of the regional accents of Scotland and certain areas of northern England (e.g. northern Lancashire and Yorkshire, Newcastle) maintain a monophthong in words like face and road, thus: [eː] and [oː].

(c) 'Post-vocalic *r*' can be heard in south-west England, parts of Lancashire, Scotland and Ireland. (Its pronunciation may have implications for the preceding vowel sound. See Appendix III.)

(d) The sound [ʌ] is not used in the north and Midlands of England. Instead, [ʊ] is generally used.

(e) The change to [ɑː] has not taken place in the north and Midlands of England.

(f) *Thou* forms can still be heard in some northern dialects, particularly Yorkshire.

The features (a), (b) and (c) can be heard in the speech of many Scottish speakers. Try listening to the Scottish recording at: http://www.ukans.edu/~idea/index2.html. Scotland 9 is a good starting point. The key to listening to accents is to focus on words containing the relevant sounds (e.g. *so, goat, coast, plain, name, Paisley,* and words with a written <r> occurring after a vowel). But also explore some of the northern England recordings on the English page of that website. While there, for (d) and (e), listen to recordings from areas like Liverpool, Manchester (and Salford) and Birmingham (Warwickshire). Also, I can strongly recommend exploring http://www.bbc.co.uk/voices/.

9.6 These areas are all sparsely populated, relative to the south-east of England. This could explain why language change has been slower here. Contact with other people is a cause of language change.

UNIT 10   STANDARDISATION

10.1 (a) The third person singular inflection -*s*, as in *walks*.
(b) *are, die, leg, want, get, both, give, same, they, them, their*.

10.2 (a) We have seen in this book that all living languages are in a constant state of change. They cannot be fixed.

(b)
1   This sentence breaks the rule that you should not end a sentence with a preposition (it ends with five!). The rule follows the conventions of Latin.
2   This sentence breaks the rule that you should not split an infinitive, i.e. *to* should immediately precede its verb (e.g. *to go* and not *to boldly go*). The rule follows Latin, in which the infinitive was just one word and thus could not be split.
3   It was (and sometimes still is) argued that *among* refers to more than two people, and thus *between* should be used here. The rule reflects the wish of some scholars to fix certain meanings to certain words (often the etymological meaning), in spite of the fact that this does not reflect what people actually do.
4   This sentence breaks the rule that you should not use a double negative, because two negatives make a positive. The rule appeals to mathematical logic. Of course, language is not a system of mathematical logic. People often use multiple negatives for a strategic purpose, such as emphasis. Nobody would understand a statement like 'We don't need no education' as expressing a positive statement, i.e. we need education. We have also seen in Unit 8 that people in the past regularly formed negative statements using multiple negatives. Today, multiple negatives are socially stigmatised.

10.3 The factors may include the following: the fact that one variety has particular prestige and is widely understood; the existence of a means for the widespread dissemination of one particular variety; the fact that one variety is given a national focus; the codification of one variety; and the adoption of one variety by the education system.

10.4 (a) The 'tyres' analogy is misleading in a number of ways. In particular, it disguises the negative side of standardisation. Standardisation means the eradication of variety – the disappearance of regional diversity. Many people see a large part of their identity as invested at a regional level.

(b) The word *standard* is used by many linguists simply to refer to a variety of language that has been standardised, i.e. that has experienced the factors given above in the answer to Exercise 10.3. In everyday language, however, it is most frequently used to mean a certain level of quality, often referring to standards of morality and behaviour. Thus, the notion of *standard language* is often seen as a kind of yardstick against which you can measure the 'quality' of people's language. Following on from this, the term *non-standard* (used by many linguists simply to refer to varieties of language, such as regional varieties, that are not part of the standard) is often taken to mean 'substandard'. It is on the basis of these misunderstandings that politicians can be frequently heard advocating the *standard* and condemning any educationalists who suggest accommodating *non-standard* varieties.

UNIT 11   WORLD ENGLISHES

11.1 (a) Some examples of ENL countries: United States, United Kingdom, Ireland, Canada, Australia, New Zealand.

(b) Some examples of ESL countries: India, Singapore, Hong Kong, Malawi, Philippines, Zimbabwe.

(c) Some examples of EFL countries: Russia, Japan, Spain, China, France, Greece.

(d) What about shifting situations? About ten years ago, I taught a student from Singapore. I asked him what his native language was, to which he replied English (with Chinese being his second language). Some ESL speakers are mainly using English with their offspring, who are then taught in English-speaking schools. Thus the new generation is shifting to ENL. What about bilinguals? Countries like India, Malta and Israel have substantial bilingual populations. What about countries with a mixed situation? South Africa, for example, has a small minority of ENL speakers, with the bulk of the population as ESL speakers.

11.2 All but the last four are from American English. Generations of my students have always got this hopelessly wrong. What they are really responding to is how new a word looks. So their thinking is: old-sounding words like *belittle* (which has been in British English since the eighteenth century) couldn't possibly be derived from American English; whereas new-sounding words like the final four (which are all first recorded in the early 1980s) must be from American English. Labelling something as American English, then, is not based on the linguistic facts. It is a negative evaluation (based on an inferiority complex? a sense of cultural threat?) principally applied to what is new.

11.4 • It is not the case that all areas of Britain use [ɑː] in these words: it is not heard in the north and Midlands of England, in Scotland or in Ireland. Conversely, in the United States [ɑː] can be heard in eastern New England, particularly around Boston.
   • Post-vocalic <r> is pronounced in some areas of Britain: in south-west England, parts of Lancashire, Scotland and Ireland. Conversely, in the United States it is not pronounced in eastern New England or the coastal areas of the southern states.
   • The merger of the vowels [ɒ] and [ɔː] is true for the area of the United States starting in Pennsylvania, extending west in a strip through the Midland states, and then spreading out to include most of the west. But it is not true for other areas. Conversely, in the British Isles many Scottish and Northern Irish speakers do not distinguish between these two vowels.
   • This seems to be generally true: *gotten* is not used in British English.
   • It is true that the word *fall* is rarely used in British English. However, *autumn* is frequently used in many varieties of American English.
   • Broadly speaking, this is accurate. However, there is some evidence that *mad* meaning 'angry' is increasing in British English, particularly among young people.

11.5

British English	American English	American English	British English
trainers	sneakers	candy	sweets
vest	undershirt	carryall	holdall
waistcoat	vest	cookie	biscuit (roughly)
motorway	expressway/ freeway	cot	camp bed

torch	flashlight	diaper	nappy
braces	suspenders	drapes	curtains
petrol	gas	faucet	tap
shop assistant	salesclerk	public school	state school

An important point to note (and one that is disguised by this exercise) is that many differences between British and American English are not a matter of simple translation, but of distribution and frequency (e.g. *diaper* also occurs in Britain, but not as frequently as *nappy*).

11.6 The speaker is a 12-year-old white girl, born in London to British-born parents. Features of London English include the use of glottal stops and the pronunciation of <l> so that it sounds more like [w]. But there are other features that are not distinctive of London. These include [ð] and [θ], as in the first sound of *the thing*, pronounced as [d] and [t]; the use of *me* as a subject pronoun; the lack of past-tense marking in *tell, see, pick* and *run*; and the use of *no* to form the negative construction *she no know what*. These features are more strongly associated with speakers living in the Caribbean, specifically in Jamaica. Here, then, there is evidence of a variety of English moving towards a creole, not the other way round. Why does this speaker have features of Jamaican English? Most of the speaker's friends are black British people, the descendants of immigrants from the West Indies. More generally, one might also note that reggae music has popularised Jamaican speech among non-Jamaican youth. And, more recently, the same might be said of Ali G, the fake hip-hop journalist. If you had guessed that this speaker came from the United States or Canada, you are not completely wrong, since immigration from the West Indies has also taken place there. Moreover, in the United States African American Vernacular English, used by many people of black African background, has some features in common with Caribbean Englishes, such as the replacement of word-initial [ð] with [d] (e.g. 'dat' for 'that'). Both varieties of English have their origins rooted in the enslavement of West Africans between the late sixteenth century and the mid-nineteenth century.

APPENDIX VI

Internet resources

PAGES OF LINKS

These websites contain links to every conceivable aspect of studying the history of English. You will also find numerous links to collections of electronically available historical texts.

http://www.towson.edu/~duncan/hellinks.html
http://www.chass.utoronto.ca/~cpercy/hell/
http://ebbs.english.vt.edu/hel/hel.html
http://www.humbul.ac.uk/english/ (try 'primary sources')

TEXTS AND IMAGES

Vast quantities of images of texts and electronic transcriptions of texts (including whole books) are now available on-line. (1) are general collection. (2) deal with ME. (3) deals with EMod.E. (4) are good for images of manuscripts.

1   http://ota.ahds.ac.uk/
     http://etext.lib.virginia.edu/english.html
     http://www.humanities.ualberta.ca/emls/emlsetxt.html
2   http://www.georgetown.edu/labyrinth/library/ME/ME.html
     http://www.hti.umich.edu/c/cme/
3   http://www.uoregon.edu/~rbear/ren.htm
4   http://image.ox.ac.uk/
     http://www.digitalmedievalist.com/rls/mss.html
     http://ibs001.colo.firstnet.net.uk/britishlibrary/controller/home
     http://sunsite.berkeley.edu/scriptorium/search/Huntington_
     search.html

DEALING WITH HANDWRITING

If you have to deal with earlier texts in English, it helps to be able to read them! These excellent websites will certainly help you cope with (and learn about) handwriting.

http://www.ualberta/ca/~sreimer/ms-course/course/ms-intro.htm
http://www.english.cam.ac.uk/ceres/ehoc

DICTIONARIES

(1) is the leading historical dictionary, the *Oxford English Dictionary*, but it is not free. (2) is the *American Heritage Dictionary of the English Language* (Boston: Houghton Mifflin, 2000); it is free and a good source of historical information. (3) are useful for the etymology of words.

1   http://www.oed.com
2   http://www.bartleby.com/61/
3   http://www.wordorigins.org.homepage.htm
     http://www.etymonline.com/
     http://www.worldwidewords.org/

PHONETICS AND GRAMMAR

The web is ideal for learning about pronunciation. (1) offers an excellent introductory guide to English phonetics, though it is limited to one accent of English – Received Pronunciation. (2) is a page of links to phonetic resources on the web. (3) is the website that accompanies Peter Ladefoged's phonetics publications. (4) is an excellent English grammar website, created by a team at University College London.

1   http://www.celt.stir.ac.uk/staff/HIGDOX/STEPHEN/
     PHONO/PHONOLG.HTM
2   http://faculty.washington.edu/dillon/PhonResources/Phon
     Resources.html
3   http://hctv.humnet.ucla.edu/departments/linguistics/Vowels
     andConsonants/
4   http://www.ucl.ac.uk/internet-grammar/

ACCENT VARIATION

(1) compare North American and British vowels and consonants. (2) contain samples of English accents. The first contains excellent samples of traditional accents/dialects, while the second is a very recent collection of samples and discussion. (3) is devoted to Estuary English.

1   http://hctv.humnet.ucla.edu/departments/linguistics/Vowels
andConsonants/course/chapter2/amerenglishvowels.html
http://faculty.washington.edu/dillon/PhonResources/newstart.
html
http://faculty.washington.edu/dillon/PhonResources/vowels.
html
2   http://www.collectbritain.co.uk/collections/dialects/
http://www.bbc.co.uk/voices
http://www.ukans.edu/~idea/
http://www.phon.ox.ac.uk/~esther/ivyweb/
3   http://www.phon.ucl.ac.uk/home/estuary/index.html

HISTORY OF ENGLISH TOPICS

(1) is the best website for OE. (2) revolves around a famous OE text, Wulfstan II's *Sermon of the Wolf to the English*, and is a good introduction to reading OE. (3) is devoted to perhaps the most famous OE text, Beowulf. (4) are excellent introductions to the languages of OE, particularly its grammar ((4) is the website relating to Peter Baker's OE book). (5) are the best websites relating to Chaucer, his work and his language. (6) are invaluable websites, focusing on the history of English sounds (the second addresses the Great Vowel Shift in particular). (7) is a fun overview of aspects of the history of English.

1   http://www.georgetown.edu/faculty/ballc/OE/old_english.html
2   http://www.cif.rochester.edu/%7Emjbernst/wulfstan/sermo_
index.html
3   http://www.humanities.mcmaster.ca/%7Ebeowulf/main.html
4   http://acunix.wheatonma.edu/mdrout/GrammarBook/KA
Grammar.html
http://www.wmich.ed/medieval/research/rawl/IOE/index.html
5   http://www.courses.fas.harvard.edu/~chaucer/
http://www.towson.edu/%7Eduncan/Chaucer/
6   http://alpha.furman.edu/~wrogers.phonemes/
http://alpha.furman.edu/~mmenzer/gvs/
7   http://www.bbc.co.uk/radio4/routesofenglish/

HISTORICAL BACKGROUND

(1) is a fun overview of aspects of British history. (2) is a comprehensive British history resource. (3) contains useful timelines and key date charts.

1   http://www.bbc.co.uk/history/lj/conquestlj/preview.shtml
2   http://www.britannia.com/history/
3   http://www.btinternet.com/~timeref/index.htm

APPENDIX VII

General reading

More advanced supplementary readings

Hogg, R.M. (series editor), *The Cambridge History of the English Language*, Cambridge: Cambridge University Press (particularly, volumes I (1992), II (1992) and III (1999), covering the Old, Middle and Early Modern English periods).

Smith, J., *An Historical Study of English: Function, Form and Change*, London: Routledge, 1996. (More concerned with the 'how' and 'why' of the history of English than the 'what'.)

Readings on the English of particular periods

Baker, P.S., *Introduction to Old English*, Oxford: Blackwell, 2003. (One of the most accessible introductions to Old English on the market.)

Burrow, J. and Turville-Petre, T. (eds), *A Book of Middle English* (3rd edn), Oxford: Blackwell, 2004. (The classic introduction to Middle English.)

Giegerich, H. (series editor), *The Edinburgh Textbooks on the English Language*, Edinburgh: Edinburgh University Press. (See especially the volumes on Old English, Middle English and Early Modern English.)

Mitchell, B. and Robinson, F., *A Guide to Old English* (6th edn), Oxford: Blackwell, 2001. (The classic introduction to Old English.)

Smith, J., *Essentials of Early English*, London: Routledge, 1999. (A clear, if perhaps a little dry, description of the linguistic characteristics of each period of English.)

Some of the many standard works on the history of the English language

Barber, C., *The English Language: A Historical Introduction*, Cambridge: Cambridge University Press, 1993.

Baugh, A. and Cable, T., *A History of the English Language* (5th edn), London: Routledge, 2002.

Pyles, T. and Algeo, J., *The Origins and Development of the English Language* (4th edn), Orlando, FL: Harcourt Brace Jovanovich, 1993.

Books that emphasize social, cultural or communicative aspects
Fennell, B., *History of English: A Sociolinguistic Approach*, Oxford: Blackwell, 2001.
Jucker, A.H., *History of English and English Historical Linguistics*, Klett: Broschiert, 2000.
Knowles, G., *A Cultural History of the English Language*, London: Arnold, 1997.
Leith, D., *A Social History of English* (2nd edn), London: Routledge, 1997.

A source book and commentary
Freeborn, D., *From Old English to Standard English* (2nd edn), London: Macmillan, 1998.

INDEX